T0323999

# Cambridge Elements ≡

**Elements in Twenty-First Century Music Practice**
edited by
Simon Zagorski-Thomas
*London College of Music, University of West London*

# WHAT MUSICKING AFFORDS

## *Musical Performance and the Post-cognitivist Turn*

Marc Duby
*University of South Africa*

**CAMBRIDGE**
UNIVERSITY PRESS

## CAMBRIDGE
### UNIVERSITY PRESS

Shaftesbury Road, Cambridge CB2 8EA, United Kingdom

One Liberty Plaza, 20th Floor, New York, NY 10006, USA

477 Williamstown Road, Port Melbourne, VIC 3207, Australia

314–321, 3rd Floor, Plot 3, Splendor Forum, Jasola District Centre,
New Delhi – 110025, India

103 Penang Road, #05–06/07, Visioncrest Commercial, Singapore 238467

Cambridge University Press is part of Cambridge University Press & Assessment,
a department of the University of Cambridge.

We share the University's mission to contribute to society through the pursuit of
education, learning and research at the highest international levels of excellence.

www.cambridge.org
Information on this title: www.cambridge.org/9781009517157

DOI: 10.1017/9781009249904

When citing this work, please include a reference to the DOI 10.1017/9781009249904

First published 2025

A catalogue record for this publication is available from the British Library

ISBN 978-1-009-51715-7 Hardback
ISBN 978-1-009-24991-1 Paperback
ISSN 2633-4585 (online)
ISSN 2633-4577 (print)

Additional resources for this publication at www.cambridge.org/Duby

# What Musicking Affords

## Musical Performance and the Post-cognitivist Turn

Elements in Twenty-First Century Music Practice

DOI: 10.1017/9781009249904
First published online: January 2025

Marc Duby
*University of South Africa*
**Author for correspondence:** Marc Duby, marcduby@me.com

**Abstract:** The last three decades of work in cognitive science have challenged the idea that thinking occurs entirely in the head, claiming instead that cognition is embodied, embedded, extended, and enactive. The claims of 4E cognition challenge the dominance of computational approaches to cognition, and music scholars have explored Gibson's notion of affordances to propose a new understanding of musical performance as primarily grounded in action. This Element draws from paradigms such as enactive cognition, cybernetic and systems-theoretical approaches, phenomenological perspectives on practice, Gibson's theory of affordances, and aspects of the author's own practice as a multi-instrumentalist to consider cases of how the interface between musician and instrument influences performance.

This Element also has a video abstract: www.cambridge.org/
EMUP_Duby_abstract

**Keywords:** musicking, ecological psychology, affordances, phenomenology of practice, enactive cognition

ISBNs: 9781009517157 (HB), 9781009249911 (PB), 9781009249904 (OC)
ISSNs: 2633-4585 (online), 2633-4577 (print)

# Contents

## Introduction

This Element is intended as a broad introductory overview of embodied cognition as applied to musical action. My aim is to provide a broad literature review which collates various strands of interdisciplinary thinking in one place, since these various theoretical approaches (and their applications) are generally somewhat scattered in the literature. This undertaking might serve emerging researchers in the field who are less than convinced that traditional computational approaches can account for musical performance as a complex phenomenon. I draw from five decades of experience engaging with various musical instruments to synthesise new ideas and insights about embodied approaches to performance and improvisation.

The last three decades of work in cognitive science have challenged the idea that thinking occurs entirely in the head, claiming instead that cognition is embodied, embedded, extended, and enactive. The claims of 4E cognition resist the dominance of computational approaches to cognition, and music scholars have explored Gibson's notion of affordances to propose a new understanding of musical performance as primarily grounded in action. I draw from paradigms such as enactive cognition, cybernetic and systems-theoretical approaches, phenomenological perspectives on practice, Gibson's theory of affordances, and aspects of my own practice as a multi-instrumentalist to consider cases of how the interface between musician and instrument influences performance.

## Outline of Contents

*The turn to embodiment* provides a general overview of post-cognitive theories (such as 4E cognition) and how these might be fruitfully applied to musical action. *The systems-theoretical turn* explores the ways in which the framework of systems theory provides insights into musical performance in the moment and over time. *The phenomenological turn* considers musicians' lived experience and their learning development over time, emphasising the connections between cognitive science and phenomenology as first-person perspective, and how these connections might be harnessed to illuminate aspects of practice. *The turn to affordances* applies Gibsonian ideas of perception and action using ecological psychology as a broad framework for revisiting musicking as grounded in action. To conclude, *the turn to practice* examines my own practices as improvising multi-instrumentalist to foreground the idea of musical action, exploring concepts such as skilled performance to frame musical activities from a first-person perspective.

## 1 Theoretical Approach: Integrative Transdisciplinarity

Lineweaver et al. (2013), while acknowledging a lack of consensus on the exact nature of complexity – 'wrestling with complexity is not a new sport', as they claim (5) – argue that 'one cannot isolate the complexity of biological organisms from the complexity of their environment' (8). The future for such biological organisms, including humankind, is far from assured, given the irreversible changes wrought by our species' wholesale exploitation of precious and irreplaceable planetary resources. Solé and Levin (2022) portray a grim picture of the current status quo, which for them requires addressing from 'a complex systems perspective':

> Confronted with a planet decline where humans are part of a complex, endangered ecological network, novel approaches need to be taken. All these approaches include unsolved, multiscale problems and will need to be applied in a social context dominated by cities, political instability and rising inequality. A complex systems perspective including all key aspects of the problem is required, pointing to an agenda of well-defined alternatives. (3)

Complex problems, at the heart of humankind's 'complex unity', demand complex solutions, and Morin (1999, cited in Montuori 2022: 167) observes that humans are 'physical, biological, psychological, cultural, social historical beings' (2), so confirming that complexity is very much part of the human condition. Hence, I believe, his call for complexification of thinking, with his conception of the physical and biological aspects of this complex human unity surely also encompassing the fact of our embodiment. Morin is alert to the operations of what he terms 'the great Western paradigm', and its accompanying binaries of subject and object, soul and body, mind and matter, and sentiment and reason, among others (9), and its consequences: 'philosophy and reflective research here, science and objective research there' (9).

From elsewhere, some cognitive scientists and psychologists[1] also understand living creatures as coterminous with their particular environments, in which they maintain themselves through mutually transforming feedback loops, within species-specific ecological 'niches', defined as 'all of the interactions of a species with the other members of its community, including competition, predation, parasitism, and mutualism. A variety of abiotic factors, such as soil type and climate, also define a species' niche'.[2]

---

[1] For instance, von Uexküll, Gibson, the enactivists, practitioners of 4E cognition, and others. What is frequently termed 'the body-brain-environment' (BBE) nexus (the *Umwelt*, in von Uexküll 2010) plays a central conceptual role in 4E cognition, ecological psychology, situated cognition, and systems theory, among other areas of research. This paradigm does not impose an artificial separation between these constituents but considers them as intertwined in mutually reinforcing feedback loops.

[2] www.britannica.com/science/niche-ecology, accessed 29 June 2023.

Montuori (2022) proposes an approach in response to Morin's concerns regarding the need for complexification. Transdisciplinary scholarship (Cronin's term) is less a method than 'a form and practice of scholarship' (163), drawing from 'empirical and theoretical research, [which] contextualizes and connects, interprets, and integrates knowledge that is often buried in specialized journals in multiple disciplines to address a particular topic'. Montuori goes on to propose an approach he calls integrative transdisciplinarity (IT), incorporating five dimensions 'as heuristics and scholarly practices to orient researchers' (163).

These dimensions include the following:

(1) understanding the world as 'interconnected, interdependent, and creative', approached from standpoints of 'systems theory and complex thought'
(2) conceiving of research undertakings as inherently creative processes
(3) led by inquiry-based rather than discipline-based methods
(4) 'meta-paradigmatic', understanding that there may be many different ways of approaching a given topic while redeploying existing theoretical frameworks
(5) 'integrating the inquirer' (second-order cybernetics), acknowledging the inquirer's viewpoint and orientation (social and psychological aspects).

Integrative transdisciplinarity understands the world as 'complex, interconnected, interdependent, and in many ways unpredictable' (164), a conception which aims to supersede the Newtonian worldview where order and deterministic rules of scientific procedure held sway. Since humans are worldly beings facing unprecedented challenges, the Newtonian view must give way to a new way of comprehending the world (163–164).

According to Montuori (2022), this emerged in the last century, drawing from 'GST,[3] Cybernetics, Information Theory, and later Chaos and Complexity theories' (166). Montuori agrees with Morin's claim that 'complexity is perhaps the greatest challenge facing humanity' (166). In order to understand pressing complex social problems, further research on 'contexts, relationships, and the social dimensions of creativity' is called for, which conceives of the individual 'as an open system in constant interaction with its environment' (166): 'Part of the challenge of complexity is to dig deeper and find the traces of powerful influences that are due to historical and cultural factors not often considered in academia – particularly when a topic is studied in a very individual-centered way – but nevertheless exert their influence in the ecology of ideas' (167).

---

[3] General systems theory: see, for instance, von Bertalanffy (1968), Jantsch (1980), Prigogine and Stengers (2017), and Luhmann (2013).

One of these powerful influences is Descartes' sundering of mind from body and the metaphysical implications of the so-called Cartesian split. This influence – and its consequences – figures prominently in mainstream academic cognitive science, and in many respects the various challenges to this picture of humanity (see note 1) are united, despite their ideological and methodological differences, in rejecting the Cartesian picture of cognition. I will return to this point later in the Element.

Yet another powerful influence concerns funding issues and institutional (corporate, military, and so on) underpinnings of research. As Penny (2017) notes, 'It is not possible to understand the form "computing" took in the late twentieth century without understanding that the majority of fundamental computing research was pursued as (US) military research with military funding. From Colossus to the Manhattan Project to the SAGE system, computing systems were developed for and framed by military agendas' (65). This dispels the assumption that research takes place in some value-free discursive space,[4] to all intents and purposes neutral and objective, sealed off from the demands and exigencies of the world beyond the laboratory walls.

The consequences of treating aspects of complex phenomena in isolation (reductionism) are reflected in academia by the increasing specialisation and fragmentation of disciplines 'with little or no communication between them' (Montuori 2022: 167). Creative inquiry aims to call into question the drawing of strict boundaries between and within disciplines that increased specialisation brings in its wake. This tendency to specialise reflects a splintering of the field into sub-disciplines,[5] academic niches into which neophytes and seasoned academics alike strive to find 'their rightful place' as (future) experts in a particular field. The fragmentation of disciplines presents a major problem when these are reduced to their constituent elements and not treated as wholes unto themselves.

For instance, specialisations in music encompass audio engineering and production, musical aesthetics, musical composition, music education, psychology of music, improvisation, jazz studies, music history, music production, sound

---

[4]  For instance, 'Much [sic] of Gibson's ideas about perception was developed during his time directing aviation training during World War II. In that context, it was critical that pilots orient themselves based on characteristics of the ground surface observed visually, rather than through data from their vestibular or kinesthetic senses' (www.newworldencyclopedia.org/entry/J._J._Gibson#Work, accessed 29 June 2023).

[5]  See von Bertalanffy (1968:51): 'Conventional education in physics, biology, psychology or the social sciences treats them as separate domains, the general trend being that increasingly smaller subdomains become separate sciences, and this process is repeated to the point that each specialty becomes a triflingly small field, unconnected with the rest.'

editing, systematic musicology, and so on.[6] This bespeaks a splintered field in which specialists abound and the musical experience is reduced to its constituent elements (melody, harmony, rhythm, pitch, and so on). To counter this tendency, Montuori (2022) proposes that 'A transdisciplinary approach may include – if pertinent to the question being researched – a range of "levels" all of which are significant in their own way. It is therefore multi-dimensional rather than reductionist' (168).

Musical phenomena, as manifested in and through performance, can be understood on many levels, as involving the physics of sound (vibrations, timbral characteristics, duration, and so on), psychosocial aspects of individual and collective agency in composing and improvising performance, broadly sociocultural concerns as to the value and purposes assigned to music in various societal formations, and its widespread nature as a worldwide practice susceptible to distribution via such technological aspects of contemporary life as the internet, social networks, and so on. Understood holistically, these musical phenomena exhibit the kind of multidimensionality Montuori claims for complex phenomena in general.

For all these reasons, I am following Montuori's lead in adopting the IT framework, in which he characterises synthesis as 'weaving together empirical research and/or ideas and theories to create new ways of understanding phenomena' (168). The various – and sometimes divergent – approaches surveyed in what follows all share to some degree the concerns of non-reductionism, the acknowledgement of embodiment as a vital factor for all manner of creatures, the dynamic changes unfolding over time through mutually reinforcing action-perception loops between environments and their inhabitants, the influence and place of the observer, and notions of ambiguity and uncertainty in a complex world. In adopting a transdisciplinary approach to questions of musical performance, I engage with these concerns 'as an embodied and embedded participant rather than spectator to life and knowledge', as Montuori (2022) characterises creative inquiry (171).

Music as experienced, traditionally conceived of as the most abstract of the performing arts,[7] regarded as a multidimensional and multisensory holistic phenomenon, encompasses aspects of affect, cognition and perception, gesture, and emotion regulation, with different purposes and ethical contexts in different cultural settings. As laboratories and repositories of knowledge, some academic

---

[6] academia.edu, accessed 19 August 2022.

[7] 'Music, the most abstract and uncanny art, is an eternal river of sound moving through time. We can free ourselves from whatever may be holding us back, and join that flowing river' (Westney 2006: 222).

approaches tend to preclude such a holistic view because their aim is analysis of the elements that constitute music, not necessarily the observer's – or the participant's, for that matter – viewpoint in performance. The distance between music as *objective knowledge* and *the experience of musical performance* is maintained, as is that between theory and practice.[8]

In regard to the differences between music understood objectively and subjectively, I find instructive parallels in Hayles' (2017) definitions of the differences between thinking and cognition. She writes: 'Thinking, as I use the term, refers to high-level mental operations such as reasoning abstractly, creating and using verbal languages, constructing mathematical theorems, composing music,[9] and the like, operations associated with higher consciousness' (14). Drawing from Maturana and Varela (1980), Hayles understands cognition, on the other hand, as 'a much broader faculty present to some degree in all biological life-forms and many technical systems'. Here she finds alignment with 'the emerging science of cognitive biology, which views all organisms as engaging in systematic acts of cognition as they interact with their environments' (14).

## 2 The Turn to Embodiment

Humberto Maturana (1928–2021) was a Chilean biologist among whose contributions to the field together with his colleague Francisco Varela (1946–2001) and others was the so-called Santiago theory of cognition. Maturana[10] independently developed this new concept of mind as process,[11] with Maturana and his colleague Francisco Varela developing Maturana's earlier work into an enactive approach to cognition. As Capra and Luisi (2014) maintain, this approach to cognition understands that 'mind and consciousness are not things

---

[8] Despite official recognition of creative outputs in South African academia (Duby 2022a), the dominance of the 'objectivist' research agenda imposes the requirement of formally stating the aims and objectives of creative work. This raises a significant problem for practitioners in articulating in verbal form the 'unthought' (Hayles 2017) actions that bring the work to fruition.

[9] Notice her conception of composition as a higher-level process, one which inadvertently conjures up an old-fashioned portrait of the composer's desk, chaotically strewn with messy ink- and coffee-stained manuscripts with a battered piano close by. I am curious as to what she might make of collective improvisation in this regard.

[10] Maturana, as one of the co-authors of Lettvin et al. (1959), collaborated with McCulloch in researching and drafting this important paper. For Hallowell (2009), 'despite the fact that some in mainstream science may view their ideas as marginal or wrong, both Maturana and Varela distinguished themselves as important, legitimate biologists through well-known laboratory work that served as the foundation for their theoretical ideas' (143).

[11] In the 1960s, the British biologist Gregory Bateson similarly argued for the notion of mind as process. 'In biology, this novel concept of mind was developed during the 1960s by Gregory Bateson, who used the term "mental process", and independently by Humberto Maturana, who focused on cognition, the process of knowing' (Capra and Luisi 2014: 252).

but processes' (252). These authors further propose that an approach to understanding real-world events as processes rather than interactions between static objects accords with developments in contemporary physics:

> Modern physics thus pictures matter not at all as passive and inert but as being in a continuous dancing and vibrating motion whose rhythmic patterns are determined by the molecular, atomic, and nuclear configurations. There is stability, but this stability is one of dynamic balance, and the further we advance into matter, the more we need to understand its dynamic nature to understand its patterns. (75)

On this post-Newtonian view, it is similarly possible to understand musical sound as an emergent *process* (Carvalho 2019), rather than some finished product. As Carvalho states it, 'We say we make music when, better put, we enact it by patterning sounds that achieve or contribute to the emergence of music in an otherwise undifferentiated field of sound' (77). For now, allow me to declare that this dynamic and emergent understanding of music making as process rings true with respect to my experience of in-the-moment performance.

As Maturana (1980: 13) suggests, the Santiago theory understands simple and complex life forms alike as cognitive systems and proposes that life and mind are themselves manifestations of cognitive processes. Capra and Luisi point out how Bateson and the Santiago theorists understood living creatures' interactions with – and within – their environments as 'cognitive', whether such organisms happen to be plants, animals, or human beings.

Von Uexküll's (2010) work on the *Umwelt* also proposes a deep connection between earthly creatures and the environments in which they live. As Capra and Luisi (2014) state it, 'Mind – or, more accurately, mental activity – is immanent in matter at all levels of life' (254). It is on this basis that Maturana can assert the apparently counter-intuitive claim that even organisms without nervous systems[12] can be understood as exhibiting forms of cognitive activity.

This approach and the later work of Maturana and Varela (also see Varela, Thompson, and Rosch 2016) examine apparently simple cases of biological cognition beginning at cellular level and find basic commonalities in all living systems, on the basis that '[a]ll known multicellular living beings are elaborate variations of the same theme: cellular organization and the constitution of a phylogeny' (1987:81). They conclude (Maturana & Varela 1998) that '[the]

---

[12] See Lagomarsino (2019, emphasis added) on tree communication, whereby 'experiments confirmed that trees are indeed communicating with each other and sharing nutrients through their roots, forming a *complex system* sometimes referred to as the "wood wide web"'. The danger of a cephalocentric model of communication is that it limits thinking to humans. It should not escape us those other modes of cognising need considering, even if they appear in 'alien' (non-human) species.

rich diversity of living beings on earth, including us, is due to the appearance of this multicellular variant within cellular lineages'.

They propose *autopoiesis* (self-making) as a principle that unites all living creatures ('autonomous, self-referring and self-constructing closed systems' (Cohen and Wartofsky 1980: v)). Jantsch (1980) acknowledges this principle as a 'core notion' in a new understanding of how living systems operate and offers the following definition: 'Autopoeisis refers to the characteristic of living systems to continuously renew themselves and to regulate this process in such a way that the integrity of their structure is maintained.[13] Whereas a machine is geared to the output of a specific product, a biological cell is primarily concerned with renewing itself' (7).

In stark contrast to this unifying framework stands the work of the French philosopher René Descartes[14] (1596–1650), who famously drew a distinction between mind and matter.

> From that I knew that I was a substance, the whole essence or nature of which is to think, and that for its existence there is no need of any place, nor does it depend on any material thing; so that this 'me', that is to say, the soul by which I am what I am, is entirely distinct from body, and is even more easy to know than is the latter; and even if body were not, the soul would not cease to be what it is.[15]

With these famous words, Descartes draws a fundamental distinction between soul as an insubstantial, eternal, and persistent entity floating free ('no need of any place') and the body as finite, transient substance, the 'material thing' par excellence. This conception of mind and matter as distinct entities (Cartesian 'substance dualism' and its later variants)[16] has permeated Western philosophy for centuries.

Proponents of embodied cognition challenge this separation between mind and its biological grounding as perpetuating an artificial distinction, one that is unproductive in attempts to understand cognition outside the confines of the laboratory. To establish the computational theory of mind (computationalism)[17]

---

[13] Complex adaptive systems (immune systems, the brain, cities, and so on) share autopoeitic principles.

[14] For a discussion of the provenance and origins of the Cartesian spilt (by way of Plato) and its implications for understanding and teaching music, see Westerlund and Juntunen (2010).

[15] Cited in Damasio (1994: 176). Also see Penny (2017: 6), who argues that 'There are historical reasons for this contorted idea – not least, Descartes's desire to reconcile his religious faith with his endorsement of emerging empirical and rationalist thought. Also he presumably wanted to avoid the fate of Giordano Bruno or Galileo.'

[16] https://plato.stanford.edu/entries/descartes/#MinRel (accessed 6 September 2022).

[17] '[Classic] CTM holds that the mind *literally is* a computing system. Of course, the most familiar artificial computing systems are made from silicon chips or similar materials, whereas the human body is made from flesh and blood. But CCTM holds that this difference disguises a more

meant treating the body as the obedient servant of the mind's instructions.[18] Damasio (1994) characterises the outcome of this paradigm as resulting in 'the separation of the most refined operations of mind from the structure and operation of a biological organism' (177).

Implicit in this conception is the idea that the brain (mind) instructs the living body to perform tasks against the background of a pre-given (static) world,[19] ideas that the theorists of the Santiago school criticise. For them, sense making,[20] in a world of perpetual movement and change and uncertainty, is a crucial part of the enactive approach in accounting for processes of dynamic change over time, one in which organisms and environments mutually adapt through cyclical action-perception loops.[21] As Jantsch (1980) presciently states it: 'Life no longer appears as a thin superstructure over a lifeless physical reality, but as an inherent principle of the dynamics of the universe' (19).

The question now arises as to which position is more appropriate for the purposes of this argument: Descartes' persistent 'I' ('the soul by which I am what I am') existing independently of bodily concerns, or the Santiago theorists' claim that mind and matter are intertwined in all living things? For Damasio (1994), 'The Cartesian idea of a disembodied mind may well have been the source, by the middle of the twentieth century, for the *metaphor of mind* as software program' (177). This idea is not confined to the computationalist paradigm but reaches far back into Western metaphysics in the form of the so-called mind–body problem, as described by Froese (2010) and Penny (2017), for instance. In the name of scientific progress, the bodily aspect of humankind was effectively excluded from the discursive frameworks and laboratory settings that undergirded the nascent disciplines of psychology and cognitive science.

---

fundamental similarity, which we can capture through a Turing-style computational model' (Rescorla 2020).

[18] 'Descartes' absolute rupture between mental and physical phenomena provided the necessary metaphysical protection for scientific activity to make progress in its quest for objectivity, while conveniently leaving the problem of subjectivity aside' (Froese 2010:76).

[19] 'Enactive cognitive science, as Varela et al. define it, is a study of mind which does not depict cognition as the internal mirroring of an objective external world. Instead, it isolates the repeated sensorimotor interactions between agent and world as the basic locus of scientific and explanatory interest' (Clark 1998:172)

[20] The notion of sense making as one of the central pillars of the enactive approach is discussed more fully later in the Element.

[21] As Fuster (2013: 90) defines this: 'A flow of environmental signals gathered by sensory systems shapes the actions of the organism upon the environment; these actions produce environmental changes, which in turn generate new sensory input, which informs new action, and so on. This circular flow of information operates in the interactions of all animal organisms with their environment.'

Notice how Damasio connects Descartes's idea to the computational theory of mind (CTM), an influential model of (largely human) cognition which arose together with the first generation of digital computers during the middle of the twentieth century. Whether conceived of as metaphor, model, or paradigm, CTM began as an ambitious research programme, to map the contours and limits of human cognition using the operations of computer software as the dominant analogy, thus conceiving of cognition as chiefly concerned with manipulating symbols in a self-contained brain.[22]

However, various critiques of CTM's disregard for embodiment began to arise from several quarters: the phenomenological tradition, ecological psychology, and, during the last decades of the twentieth century, theories of embodied (4E) cognition. In addition, from cybernetics and dynamical systems theory came techniques for measuring phenomena whose nature and behaviour change in and over time.

For Stewart (2014: 1 ff.), Cartesian dualism treats animals as machines, so that the CTM naturally tends to privilege human over animal cognition.[23] As before, the enactive paradigm postulates a broader connection between matter and living creatures. Maturana's 1970 essay on the biology of cognition (in Maturana & Varela 1980) grounds his early work in cognition in the biology of living systems in asserting that 'The observer is a living system and an understanding of *cognition as a biological phenomenon* must account for the observer[24] and his role in it' (9, emphasis added).

One of the main tenets of 4E cognition (Newen et al. 2018) is that all living creatures interact with environments through exploratory actions in mutually influential fashion. Understanding these interactions must take account of factors such as environmental coupling (Penny 2017) and sensorimotor contingencies (Noë 2015) to provide a robust and ecologically valid account of real-world cognitive processes. Stewart (2014) points out that 'enaction takes first-person lived experience, and in particular the phenomena of consciousness,[25] far more seriously than does the computational paradigm' (4).

To take account of lived experience in this fashion is a far cry from CTM's understanding of cognition as the manipulation of symbols inside the human

---

[22] This conception implies the existence of mental representations (symbols) and a cephalocentric understanding of cognition based in rationality.

[23] This is in contrast to the Santiago theorists' emphasis on the continuity of cognition between and across different species.

[24] This idea of the observer is the harbinger of second-order cybernetics, discussed more fully later in the Element.

[25] Consciousness, for Hayles (2017: 52), 'is not the whole of cognition, and ... nonconscious cognition is especially important in environments rich in complex information stimuli'.

brain. In so doing, adherents of CTM placed human beings at the top of the tree of knowledge, consigning animal cognition to being something of mere curiosity value. In other words, animal cognition was construed as running on a far simpler software program than its human counterpart. While it is true that human cognition exhibits far greater complexity than that of the animal kingdom, it seems mistaken simply to ignore instances of animal cognition as a basis of comparison.

Also see Stewart et al. (2014), where Stewart argues that 'the paradigm of enaction is very naturally able to take into account the bulk of the social and human sciences, notably anthropology, by examining the processes of hominization that made the link between animal worlds and human worlds' (4 ff.). Enactivists, at least in this instance, postulate a connection between these worlds that CTM ignores.

In this regard, Barrett's (2015) work on avian cognition (83–84) provides a cautionary tale with respect to human tendencies to anthropomorphise animal actions. The weaver bird provides a telling example. Because their nests show universal design features, it is tempting to assume that these characteristics draw from some hereditary template (or avian blueprint) to which all weaver birds have access through genetic inheritance, for argument's sake.

However, Barrett shows that this assumption is flawed. The original experiments conducted by John Crook in the 1960s (where he would remove part of the nest while the birds were constructing it) revealed that 'the birds that build these delightful objects have no overall concept or sense of their own design' (83). For Barrett, the birds' actions are explicable in terms of simple heuristics and not executed according to some 'pre-formed plan inside the birds' heads' (84). A certain element of caution, it seems, is necessary to avoid ascribing human intentions to different species.

Di Paolo, Rohde, and De Jaegher (2014) list five essential elements of enactivism, understood as 'a kind of nonreductive, nonfunctional naturalism', (36): autonomy, sense making, emergence, embodiment, and experience. Taking these essential components of enactivism in order, autonomy is instantiated (37) by creatures conforming with laws which their own activities generate. These activities depend, in turn, on structural animal–environment couplings: 'Cognitive systems are also autonomous in an interactive sense in terms of their engagement as agents and not simply as systems coupled with other systems' (38).[26]

---

[26] In similar fashion, Casasanto (in Shapiro 2019: 80) proposes the 'body-specificity hypothesis', stated simply as 'people with different kinds of bodies think differently'.

Sense making, as the second pillar of enactivism, is inherently *active*. 'For the enactivist, sense is not an invariant[27] present in the environment that must be retrieved by direct (or indirect) means. Invariants are instead the outcome of the dialogue between the active principles of organisms in action and the dynamics of the environment' (39). Through this action-grounded dialogue, organisms bring forth – or *enact* – a world. Further to this point, they define sense making as 'the evaluation of the consequences of interaction for the conservation of an identity' (45).

They characterise emergence as 'the formation of a novel property or process out of the interaction of different existing processes or events' (40). They categorise 'life itself' (41) as quintessentially emergent insofar as a new level of identity emerges from interactions within 'a self-sustaining bounded network of chemical transformations' (41). Regarding the notion of emergence, Capra and Luisi (2014) include music theory in the list of fields which draw from this concept: 'In our time, emergence is being considered not only in chemistry and biology but also in quite a variety of other research fields, such as cybernetics, artificial intelligence, nonlinear dynamics, information theory, social science, and the theory of music (the harmony arising from a musical phrase is obviously not present in the single notes)' (155).

'In a concrete and practical sense, a cognitive system is embodied to the extent to which its activity depends nontrivially on the body' (Di Paolo et al. 2014: 42). For Di Paolo, Rohde, and De Jaegher, regarding the body as 'an information-processing device' falls back into the Cartesian error by separating mind as function from body as implementation. Again, taking account of sense making, they conclude that cognition on this view *can only be embodied*. Similarly, for Cassam (2011), 'To conceive of a disembodied being is to conceive of a being with no sensorimotor knowledge and no bodily skills. Such a being could not be a perceiver and its knowledge of the world could not be perceptual knowledge' (153).

Drawing further from work in cognitive linguistics, Di Paolo, Rohde, and De Jaegher claim that notions of embodiment, far from being limited to the realm of the sensorimotor, also include so-called higher cognitive functions (reasoning, language use, and so on) because these are structured by specific bodies in coupling with specific environments. Hence, higher functions also form part of the sense making of creatures enacting worlds in real time and cannot be restricted to the manipulation of arbitrary symbols within brains as CTM claims.

---

[27] The notion of invariants comes from ecological psychology with the attendant claim that invariant properties of environments are directly perceived.

Finally, Di Paolo, Rohde, and De Jaegher (2014) argue the centrality of experience for the enactivist paradigm. 'Far from being an epiphenomenon or a puzzle as it is for cognitivism, experience in the enactive approach is inter-twined with being alive and immersed in a world of significance' (43). So saying, they emphasise that which CTM does not, or cannot, account for: experience beyond (and irreducible to) measurable data. They point out how the kind of experience which develops as skilled practitioners learn their craft is more correctly characterised as transformation than as information (44). In the sense that developing expertise in a field relies on 'non-representational skill acquisition' (Dreyfus 2002), they claim that such expertise is self-transforming and that false starts, errors, and experimentation play a vital part in 'a lawful relation of bodily and experience transformations' (44).

## 2.1 Enactive Cognising and (Artistic) Practice

For enactivists such as Noë (2004), 'perceiving is something we do rather than something that happens to us' (1, cited in Cassam 2011: 153). So, it is possible after all that our perceptions of 'things as they are' in a dynamic, ever-changing world might be illusory or mistaken, hence the numerous examples in the psychology literature of the fallibility of perceptions.[28]

Enactivists tend to disagree on the status of the relationship between percep-tion, embodied skills, and sensorimotor knowledge, with some claiming that the relationship is causal (what we might term 'weak' enactivism), others that it is constitutive (the 'strong' version). The strong version understands perception as a skilful and creative activity grounded in movement and interaction in a dynamic context, but both versions understand processes of perception as *influenced by* (weak version) or *constituted by* (strong version) creaturely embodiment. Cognition operates by way of perception–action cycles[29] and through structural coupling between moving organisms and dynamic environments.

Penny (2017) maintains that 'art and cultural practices epitomize the sorts of intelligent action that have remained inadequately addressed by the reigning

---

[28] The psychology literature abounds with various examples of unreliable perception, such as the rubber hand illusion (DeNora 2014: 118–121), the blind spot, and so on. These cases suggest that sense making is not infallible, and the perceiver can be deceived. See also Pacherie (2018: 375): 'In each case, there is a divergence between what subjects consciously see and their visually guided behavior, suggesting that the spatial information used for visually guided action and the (illusory) spatial content of conscious visual experience might be processed relatively independently.'

[29] 'The cycle is made of the circular cybernetic flow of information between the environment, sensory structures, and motor structures' (Fuster 2010: 831). Aspects of cybernetics and its implications for CTM and enactivism are discussed later in this Element.

paradigm of cognition of the later twentieth century' (13). The roots of the former dominance of CTM go deep, as he argues, because this dominance within academia served to marginalise all kinds of practices which did not – or would not – align themselves with CTM's emphasis on symbol manipulation within an isolated brain. While CTM reigned supreme, there was no room for wide-ranging conceptions of cognition in and as action, as enactivism and its related approaches (broadly speaking, embodied knowing) propose. The effects of this dominance for the so-called 'knowledge economy' were felt in academia across disciplines specialising in understanding art and cultural practices, by the performing arts specifically.

The purpose of this introductory overview to enactive cognition was to suggest that the CTM framework cannot account for real-time musical inter-actions. Musicking (Small 1998) aligns better with an enactive framework for two main reasons. First, perceiving music is not purely 'rational' in any sense of the term because it encompasses the whole body, encompassing procedural knowledge ('how to play an instrument'). *Analysing* 'the music' in terms of its individual elements (melody, harmony, rhythm, and so on) differs from *experiencing* music holistically. For it is not musical brains which engage with it but musical bodies conjoined with brains[30] in specific environments, in which the character of reception may vary from rational, emotional, visceral, physical, or admixtures of these elements. For instance, at high volume levels musical sounds become more obviously physical, when, for instance, low-frequency sounds are not only heard but felt in the chest or gut.

Second, it is the nature of CTM to limit its field of inquiry to what takes place inside people's heads. While CTM's adherents do not entirely deny the body's existence, they do not consider how hands – and feet – shape musical perform-ance. It is little wonder, then, that considering performance solely according to its intellectual content effectively excludes the here and now of performance in the moment it enters the world because the character of musical knowledge as manifested in performance is pre-verbal. An enactive approach seems better suited to capture what practitioners actually do (drawing from procedural knowledge) as opposed to what they (or researchers) say they do (declarative knowledge) (see Dowling 1993).

The necessity of embodiment for situated cognition may seem self-evident to some critics of CTM, and in this regard Robbins and Aydede (2009) draw an important distinction between on-line and off-line processing. They write:

---

[30] 'Cognition and emotion are not realized in the brain but with a brain; that is, to think and to feel, we need more than a brain. Brain regions work in concert, but they are never alone; rather, they are always parts of broader systems extending beyond skin and skull' (Malafouris 2020: 4). Gallagher (2009) makes the related claim that 'situated cognition cannot be disembodied' (35).

On-line sensorimotor processing occurs when we actively engage with the current task environment, taking in sensory input and producing motor output. Off-line processing occurs when we disengage from the environment to plan, reminisce, speculate, daydream, or otherwise think beyond the confines of the here and now. The distinction is important, because only in the on-line case is it plausible that sensorimotor capacities are body dependent. For off-line functioning, presumably[31] all one needs is a working brain. (4)

For the purposes of what follows and specifically with respect to practice, it may also be useful to draw an artificial line between cognition (high-level, catch-all category) and learning as a subset of the broader term. There are two reasons for drawing this imaginary line: First, cognition is complex and multi-faceted (drawing from memory, knowledge, and so on). Second, to head off the idea of the noun 'cognition' as somehow a static thing (akin to a bank or repository of knowledge into which is deposited accumulations of cultural capital), the point of emphasis here is that cognising is *a dynamic process of interaction between embodied agents in specific environments*. That said, the commonly accepted term in the literature is 'cognition', as in 4E, distributed, social, (and so on) cognition. It seems to me that 'embodied cognising' more aptly captures the dynamic nature of these processes.

The centrality of embodiment to practice (Smith & Dean 2009) is a no-brainer[32] for artisans, performing artists, sportspeople (gymnasts, track and field athletes, soccer players), and so on. In the most general terms, these groups of people display the most immediately obvious characteristics of on-line situated learning[33] (engagement with 'the current task environment,' as earlier), as related to the learning processes of specific individuals, times, and places. If it's plausible that learning is socially situated ('no person is an island'), it follows that communities of practice have a vital role to play in socialising learning with regard to the actual sites where these communities find themselves. Here's an example to clarify this line of argument.

---

[31] This distinction neatly encapsulates the difference between action and reflection upon action, key constituents of practice (as, -led, -based) research. Robbins and Aydede's use of 'presumably' gives the game away as a *reductio ad absurdum* (the famous 'brain in a vat' counterargument of philosophy of mind).

[32] Mild pun intended, but this claim is nonetheless crucial to what follows.

[33] 'We rejected the notion of learners as immobile recipients of information, instead focusing on centripetal movement, changing locations and ways of participating, and a notion of how knowledgeability changes in these circumstances. We suggested that value (complexly, contradictorily, positive and negative) is created by/for all participants through their engagements in practice. 'Identity' was a concept whose purpose was to insist that increasing knowledgeable skill is only a small part of the broader social being of newcomers becoming old-timers' (Lave 2008: 285–286).

I've long been puzzled as to why neuroscientists, for example, can make claims such as this one: 'We begin this chapter with the bold claim that it provides a neuroscientific explanation of the magic of creativity' (Gabora & Ranjan 2013: 19). Clearly, it's an attention-getting, even arresting, opening gambit from which colleagues in 4E cognition might recoil in horror. The reader might fairly conclude that I find such a claim mildly absurd – which I certainly do – but before I essentialise the opponent ('Oh, they're just neuroscientists; what could they possibly understand about embodiment?'), I want to consider my own reaction to this statement and my qualifications in rejecting this claim out of hand.

To begin with, let us take seriously the idea that communities of practice coalesce around the term 'practice.' The implication is that writing about practice emanates from a specific context: in this case, perhaps a research institute or an operating theatre. So, it's not just about what these authors put to paper but how the entirety of their site of practice (their professional milieu) shapes what they do in their working lives and in turn how they document their findings. Here I have in mind how neuroscientists might use a specific set of tools (protocols, operating procedures, and techniques) in their daily doings.

What I'm trying to achieve here is to account for a vexing question: why do neuroscientists apparently ignore (or reject outright) the embodiment thesis? I think the answer lies in the *Umwelt* in which such research unfolds and has to do with the kind of tools and discursive 'units of meaning' commonly available within such *Umwelt*s. So, for instance, neuroscientists might well deal in neurons as their unit of currency, neurosurgeons in lesions, economists in actual currency, and so forth. If your working environment encourages a focus on neuronal activity, you might depend on fMRI scans as evidence to provide 'a neurological explanation' which differs from that of a neurosurgeon whose focus might be surgical interventions to assist in rehabilitating a stroke patient, and so on.

It takes a certain amount of philosophical acumen to view the patient less as an immediate problem-solving challenge than from a wider perspective which incorporates the patient's immediate needs as well as the philosophical implications of their condition, to zoom out from the tree to take in the forest. How people make their way in the world, what they learn from their daily activities and interactions with colleagues, surely must shape their thought processes, their areas of research interests, and paradigms accordingly.

While I myself would very much prefer someone investigating my physical brain with a view to surgery to be qualified in all senses to do so, their expertise as a specialist neurosurgeon might well blind them to what lies outside their daily professional frame of reference. It seems uncontroversial to state that the path of specialisation narrowly constrains the specialist's focus (once again, in accordance with their professional milieu in the context of their chosen community of practice). So, a neuroscientist's perspective might well condition her to exclude certain possibilities which lie beyond her field of interest.

If these authors had indeed addressed 'the magic of creativity' at neuronal level, there would be much rejoicing at the elimination of this vexed question. As a musician by profession, I would be relieved that a neuronal account managed effectively to eliminate broader philosophical questions of creativity. I say this because creativity cannot be located at a particular level of activity in the brain unless one ignores the BBE paradigm. There is a conflict between neuroscientific and philosophical accounts of creativity that lies, as before, in the different communities of practice in which these accounts (together with their associated discursive frameworks, tools, and research techniques) reside. So that while the neuroscientist and her colleague in philosophy might be discussing the same topic (creativity and the brain, in this case), they are actually speaking different languages in doing so.

## 2.2 Embodied Cognising and Musical Meaning

Turning to notions of musical meaning, a growing body of literature on musical performance (among which are Iyer 2002; Clarke 2005; Lesaffre, Maes, and Leman 2017; and Kim & Gilman 2018) proposes that understanding the complexities of such performance needs to take account of human embodiment. Authors in 4E cognition differ quite substantially on the details and warrants of their respective claims but might well agree with the broad claim that embodiment is crucial to musical cognition and perception.

For music scholars, embodied cognising represents a new paradigm for exploring musical performance which challenges the orthodoxy of brain-based approaches to understanding music perception and cognition. This orthodoxy ignores musical actions by flesh and blood humans, whether engaged in dancing, performing, or listening, all of which entail the presence of human agents as a condition of possibility.

For the purposes of this argument, I lay out a conception of music as activity, following Small's (1998) well-known definition of 'musicking'.[34] Small defined this term fairly widely: 'To music is to take part, in any capacity,

---

[34] See Raimondi (2019) for an account of Maturana's use of the similar usage of 'languaging' (1983). While this usage antedates Small's book, it's less clear to me whether or not Small was aware of this. Raimondi (2019) argues that 'Despite the lack of a unanimous definition of languaging, most of the scholars aim to overcome the traditional, reified conception of language while embracing an alternative, non-cognitivist paradigm of cognition' (19). It seems to me that Small's intent with 'musicking' has a similar aim.

whether by performing, by listening, by rehearsing or practising, by providing material for performance (which is called composing), or by dancing' (9). Granted that 'the music'[35] as noun exists in many contexts, Small's insights foreshadow to some degree many of the concerns expressed in more contemporary musicological accounts which place the emphasis on musicking[36] as an activity.

First, we notice his neologism, 'to music'. The notion of music has shifted from noun (object) to verb (activity) whereby participation in this activity ('in any capacity') encompasses a wide range of musical actions from performance through listening to rehearsing, composing, and dancing. Second, Small's vision is inclusive by implication, making no distinctions between the virtuoso and the novice, the soloist and the ensemble, or the listener and the dancer, for example. His is an egalitarian position, seeking to avoid entrenched hierarchies between participants in the musicking process. Finally, Small's idea of 'composing' as simply 'providing material for performance' leaves open the purpose of the material or its complexity, so calling into question the entrenched idea (at least, in the West) of the composer as lone genius.[37]

Small (1998) goes on to describe the less obvious connections that enable such activities: for professional performers, these might include networks including sound engineers, FOH staff, road managers, publicists, record company executives, and so on. Together with his emphasis on musical activity as an appropriate agenda goes his notion that musicking enacts relationships, intimate or distant as they may be: 'The act of musicking establishes in the place where it is happening a set of relationships, and it is in those relationships that the meaning of the act lies' (13). So, saying, Small points beyond the music itself and infra-musical note-to-note meanings to the human beings who model ideal relationships in and through their participation in the unfolding musical processes.

Taken together, these implications of musicking as *activity* presuppose a body – or more precisely, a group of embodied individuals – as a point of origin. Participating in musicking, whether as performers, listeners, composers, or dancers implies participating in an *embodied ritual*, one in which it is difficult to take part without some minimal bodily activity. As Small (1998) maintains, 'In all those activities we call the arts, we think with our bodies. They negate with every gesture the Cartesian split between body and mind' (140).

---

[35] In colloquial parlance, one hears this term often enough, whether referring to sheet music for an upcoming performance or artefacts of recorded music (LP records, CDs, and so on).

[36] See also Malafouris' (2020) use of the term 'thinging'.

[37] Whyton (2010: 11) finds parallels with the exaltation of the Western composer in the jazz tradition, where 'we are led to believe that jazz icons transcend the very music they have created'.

In similar fashion, Johnson (2007) maintains that '[t]he meaning in and of the music is not verbal or linguistic, but rather bodily and felt' (242). Feeling the music bodily is a radical shift from the detached analysis of musical scores as purported conduits of the composer's intentions.

Johnson (2007) argues that 'music is meaningful because it can present the flow of human experience, feeling, and thinking in concrete, embodied forms – and this is meaning in its deepest sense' (236). In his understanding, the octave leap which opens Judy Garland's original 1939 rendition of *Over the Rainbow*[38] ('Some-where') enacts tension[39] by virtue of 'the strain and increased energy required to reach the higher note' (240).

As listeners, we understand this tension partly through imagining or feeling the singer's greater physical effort in producing the higher Eb, so pointing to heightened emotions, which Johnson characterises in this case as portraying a sense of longing. From another quarter, Langer (1948) describes the relation-ship between musical structure and human emotions as built on the analogous commonalities between this structure and what she describes as 'the forms of human feeling'. She writes:

> The tonal structures we call 'music' bear a close logical similarity to the forms of human feeling – forms of growth and of attenuation, flowing and stowing, conflict and resolution, speed, arrest, terrific excitement, calm, or subtle activation and dreamy lapses – not joy and sorrow perhaps, but the poignancy of either and both – the greatness and brevity and eternal passing of everything vitally felt. Such is the pattern, or logical form, of sentience; and the pattern of music is that same form worked out in pure, measured sound and silence. Music is a tonal analogue of emotive life. (27)

For Johnson, writing nearly fifty years later, the operations of what Langer terms this 'tonal analogue' between music and life are grounded in human embodiment and the metaphorical structures within which human languaging arises and operates. It is understandable that Langer stops short of making outright claims regarding embodiment because her thoughts antedate the estab-lishment of cognitive science as a standalone discipline. It seems, though, that Johnson (2007) understands and accepts her proposal of 'expressive form'[40] as the guiding force behind musical understanding (238–239).

---

[38] www.youtube.com/watch?v=oW2QZ7KuaxA, accessed 30 September 2022.

[39] Drawing from Bergson, Kahn (2017) argues that 'the very fact of sounds being high or low have [sic] to do with bodily location' (49). In other words, there is a direct correlation between a given note's pitch and where the singer places it in her body.

[40] Langer (1948) characterises 'A work of art [as] an expressive form created for our perception through sense or imagination, [expressing] human feeling' (15). Her definition of feeling (15) ranges from 'physical sensation, pain and comfort, excitement and repose' to 'the most complex emotions, intellectual tensions, or the steady feeling-tones of a conscious human life'.

As a thought experiment, it may be worth considering what meaningful change might obtain from inverting the first interval of the song to produce a descending octave. The version of 'Over the Rainbow' by the British jazz composer Django Bates (1998) presents a quite different soundscape,[41] with Iain Ballamy's tenor saxophone repeating the opening octave figure in the introduction before the vocal entry. Heavily processed electric piano and other keyboards, birdsong, and Bates' distant voice form the background to Josefine Cronhølm's deadpan[42] vocal delivery.

Clearly, Johnson's analysis diverges from its music-syntactical or music-semantic counterparts by placing the locus of analysis in the singer's embodied activity and our similarly embodied responses to this activity as people listening to or watching (in either case, *experiencing*) the performance. In the film version, captured when Garland was sixteen years old, visual cues abound, such as her wistful expression and the deserted farmyard, together with the dialogue immediately preceding the song where the young Dorothy speaks of 'a place far, far away'. While the lyrics and *mise-en-scène* may well influence the listener's sense making in this case, consider this claim by Swanwick (2007):

> The same fundamental metaphorical processes are at work in all music. Sounds are heard as expressive gestures; these gestures are transformed into new relationships. *In this dynamic and open way music appears almost to have a life of its own.* The creation of new relationships lies at the heart of what is called musical form, an organic process involving the relocation of musical ideas in new contexts, essentially metaphorical. (500, emphasis added)

Notice how Swanwick refers to sounds in general, leaving it to the reader's discretion to gauge the influence of lyrics if and when they appear. Thus, the listener's decision as to what makes such sounds meaningful is not entirely free from cultural constraints which might lead to misinterpretation. By this statement I simply mean that perceiving and understanding such relationships depends on the listener's cultural background and consequent familiarity (or lack thereof) with the conventions on which the music is built.

So, it is possible that one might encounter music that is entirely unfamiliar, not only in terms of what it immediately presents in its sonic makeup/character/content but with regard to its social and ethical underpinnings. In principle, Swanwick's account of music perception – depending on metaphor, gesture, and

---

[41] As does Tuck Andress' version (1990), which fuses *Over the Rainbow* and *If I Only had a Brain* in a technical and musical tour de force. For a transcription, see https://static1.squarespace.com/static/5a5bd42e8fd4d2aea7b0b426/t/5eb19eeb0293c02a173d1437/1588698876074/Rainbow.pdf, accessed 19 May 2023.

[42] Deadpan, in the sense that she deploys very little vibrato.

relationships – appears to float free from such possible errors of interpretation, so while the processes of meaning-making may be similar across culture, the musical content and the nuances of its meaning may well not.

## 3 The Systems-Theoretical Turn (Cybernetics 101)

The Macy conferences on cybernetics (1943–1954)[43] consisted of a foundational series of meetings involving luminaries in the fields of information theory (Claude Shannon), neuroscience (Warren McCulloch), computing (John von Neumann), and cybernetics itself (Norbert Wiener, the instigator of the cybernetic project). Their aim was to draft a new theory concerning humankind's relationship to technology (various instantiations of 'machines'). Informed by a triumvirate of core concerns (information, control, and communication), cybernetics is 'concerned with those properties of systems that are independent of their concrete material or components', making room for descriptions of 'very different systems, such as electronic circuits, brains, and organizations, with the same concepts, and to look for isomorphisms between them' (Heylighen & Joslyn 2001: 6).

Over time, cybernetics develops from first-order cybernetics (understanding complex machines as 'things') to second-order cybernetics (the 'cybernetics of cybernetics', which takes account of the observer's position through the concept of reflexivity). As Von Foerster (2003) states it: 'the cybernetician, by entering his own domain, has to account for his or her own activity. Cybernetics then becomes cybernetics of cybernetics, or *second-order cybernetics*' (289).

Froese (2010) traces the historical origins of CTM and the enactive paradigm to the cybernetics movement of the 1940s and 1950s. He draws a comparison between first-order cybernetics, based on the concept of 'mind as mechanism,' and CTM, explaining how the later wave of second-order cybernetics, whose tenet was the inclusion of the observer, gave birth to enactivism.

The shift from the core concept of homeostasis (self-maintenance) to reflexivity,[44] for Hayles, ushers in the second wave of cybernetics, fully realised with the 1980 publication by Maturana and Varela of *Autopoeisis and Cognition*, wherein 'the two authors expanded the reflexive turn into a fully articulated epistemology that sees the world as a set of informationally closed systems. Organisms respond to their environment in ways determined by their

---

[43] See Hayles (1999: 50–83) for a fine-grained discussion of the intellectual debates and interpersonal dynamics at play in this 'breathtaking enterprise,' as she describes it (7).

[44] Hayles (1999) defines reflexivity as 'the movement whereby that which has been used to generate a system is made, through a changed perspective, to become part of the system it generates' (8).

internal self-organization. Their one and only goal is continually to produce and reproduce the organization that defines them as systems. Hence, they not only are self-organizing but also are autopoeitic, or self-making' (Hayles 1999: 10). For Froese, the break between first- and second-order cybernetics is decisive in the establishment of mainstream cognitive science as the computationalist child of the former, with the enactive paradigm carrying the latter forward.

Returning to the Macy conferences, later attendees included Heinz von Foerster (one of the founders of second-order cybernetics, as noted earlier), the anthropologist Margaret Mead, and Gregory Bateson, the theoretical foundations of whose work Small (1998) discusses in an interlude (50–63). Regarding the type of information all living creatures need to transmit and receive to maintain their living conditions (a cybernetic question, if ever there was), Small (1998) writes:

> Bateson's answer is that although the means of communication are extremely varied, *what is necessary for an organism to know always concerns a relationship*: how the perceiving creature relates to the outside entity that is being perceived, and vice versa. Is it predator, for example, is it prey, is it offspring or a potential mate? And thus should I flee it, or attack it, or nurture it, or mate with it? It is clearly of vital importance for the creature to have the right answers to these questions. (56, emphasis added)

Cybernetic concepts[45] provide a link between the Batesonian influence on Small's thinking about musicking as activity, seen in Small's use of the term 'relationship.' Relation and distinction, as central methodological constructs in the cybernetic project, are abstractions, because, as we have seen, cybernetics disregards actual material properties in search of consistent aspects of similarity and difference across various contexts. With regard to 'the corporeal interplay' in musical performance, Tanaka and Donnarumma (2018: 79ff) maintain that this 'interlocking of acoustic and body physiology takes on a phenomenological dimension and can be thought of as *a cybernetic human-machine extended system*' (80, added emphasis). Both these authors and Small, it seems, are aligned in adopting second-order cybernetic thinking, wherein human agency is factored back into the equation.[46]

---

[45] Referring to cybernetic concepts of order, complexity, hierarchy, and structure, among others, Heylighen and Joslyn (2001) suggest that these are all '*relational*, in that they allow us to analyze and formally model different abstract properties of systems and their dynamics, for example allowing us to ask such questions as whether complexity tends to increase with time' (6, original emphases).

[46] Heylighen et al. (2017) note that 'we, as observers, are also cybernetic systems. This means that *our knowledge is a subjective construction, not an objective reflection of reality*' (123, emphasis added).

Noting that for Heylighen and Joslyn (2001: 3), 'Cybernetics had from the beginning been interested in the similarities between autonomous, living systems and machines,' one can draw distinct parallels between these concerns of early cybernetics and human beings, understood as 'systems of systems'. By this I mean that the physiology of the human body houses interlocking systemic aspects, susceptible to conception as systems within systems. What, then, constitutes such systems in general terms?

## 3.1 Defining Systems

To define systems, Turvey (2009) begins by describing the characteristics of a *nonsystem*, understood as 'a collection of related pieces where the relations have no implications for the properties or behaviors of the pieces. Certainly, lacking in the image of a nonsystem is the sense of shared influences or mutual dependencies; intuitively, a nonsystem exhibits no coherence or functional unity' (99). Turvey's definition raises the question of what a musical nonsystem might resemble and what kinds of 'coherence' or 'unity' might be lacking in such a (non)system. Perhaps the closest thing to such a phenomenon might be found within fields such as free jazz[47] or experimental music, where relational possibilities (imitation of an antecedent phrase, for instance) might be avoided as deliberate aesthetic strategies.

Systems differ from aggregates or heaps in that changing one element in a system significantly alters its overall performance. With regard to living systems, consider the example of a soccer game in which a player is red-carded for an offence, so reducing the overall number of players in the team.[48] In systems terms, this represents a perturbation to which the system is bound to respond, either adaptively (evolving) or by becoming dysfunctional (facing defeat or extinction). As related to live ensemble performance, one thinks of the wide range of unexpected eventualities[49] that can work against a successful performance outcome (Duby 2022b).

The systems model encompasses a vast range of scale and complexity – from molecules to galaxies, from microbes to human bodies. As Meadows (2008) defines it:

---

[47] See Borgo (2022) for an exhaustive application of systems theory to free improvisation. See also Crispell (2002).

[48] This example leans on Vlassis' (2022) description of a robotic soccer team. He writes (4): 'Robot soccer provides a testbed where MAS [multiagent systems] algorithms can be tested, and where many real-world characteristics are present: the domain is continuous and dynamic, the behavior of the opponents may be difficult to predict, there is uncertainty in the sensor signals, etc.'

[49] See Duby (2020) for an understanding of musical ensembles as systems and Duby (2022b) for an account of real-world challenges which may affect ensemble live performance.

> A school is a system. So is a city, and a factory, and a corporation, and a national economy. An animal is a system. A tree is a system, and a forest is a larger system that encompasses subsystems of trees and animals. The earth is a system. So is the solar system; so is a galaxy. Systems can be embedded in systems, which are embedded in yet other systems. (290)

For her, systems must include related 'elements, interconnections, and a function or purpose'. As related to musical performance, the function of an ensemble is to musick to the best of its abilities, its interconnections are the social and musical relationships brought to life in and through performance, and the performers' embodied actions represent its constituent elements.

Capra and Luisi (2014) similarly emphasise patterns of interconnection as the driving force of biological self-organisation: 'What is destroyed when a living organism is dissected is its pattern. The components are still there, but the configuration of relationships between them – the pattern – is destroyed, and thus the organism dies' (94). The human body – made up of multi-modal interconnected systems – serves as an exemplar of Meadows' embedded systems, from the skin (as both container and boundary) all the way down to the chemical reactions that enable autopoeisis. Gibson (1966) considers the senses (basic orienting, auditory, haptic, haptic-somatic, taste, smell, and visual) as perceptual *systems*, facilitating discovery through the sense-making organism's actions (as 'detection') rather than as merely passive receivers of information.

Understood as cognitive systems – particularly 'as complex non-linear[50] dynamical systems that may interact at various stages of development' (Marin and Peltzer-Karpf, 2009: 284) – language and music as acoustic phenomena have yielded rich data in a long and fertile relationship with the natural sciences. Music with its 'floating intentionality' (Cross 2007: 655) draws from the fields of mathematics, physics, acoustics, linguistics, musicology, technology, and so on. For the purposes of this argument, the emphasis is placed on musical performance as a cognitively complex achievement, in keeping with this claim by Zatorre and colleagues: Musical performance's demands on 'memory and motor control capabilities make expert music performance a useful domain in which to study the human brain' (Brown, Zatorre, & Penhune 2015: 57–58).

When applied to musical cognition in performance as a 'cultural' phenomenon,[51] however, systems thinking operates at a level of analysis where the specific genre conventions of a given musical practice are less

---

[50] 'A relationship between two elements in a system where the cause does not produce a proportional (straight-line) effect' (Marin and Peltzer-Karpf 2009: 284).

[51] According to ecological psychology, the boundary lines between human and animal (and human and robot) may be less clear than we assume, because many sentient creatures share body-brain-environment systems (von Uexküll, 2010) .

significant to the discussion than the large-scale operations of the system as an interconnected whole. This focus suggests that while DST is particularly applicable to improvised musicking (Borgo 2022), its tenets can be applied to all musicking, when the emphasis is placed on process over product.

To consider live performances as demonstrations of cognitive systems at work – while taking note of the wide range of expression and purpose of performance in diverse cultural contexts – aims to bracket out aesthetic issues of normativity about musical content to bring a sharper focus to bear on musical performance as a cognitive system, and how musical affordances give rise to emergent processes within performance.

A fundamental advantage in adopting a systems approach to musicking is to avoid the potential trap of reductionism. As characterised by Zhang and Patel (2006), reductionism holds that 'the cognitive properties of a group can be entirely determined by the properties of individuals. In this view, to understand group behavior, all we need is to understand the properties of individuals' (335). In other words, this approach understands the properties of this group by adopting a linear approach, in which the behaviour of individuals is understood additively; collective actions add up to the final result.

By analogy, common household salt (NaCl) is understood as consisting of a particular combination of sodium and chlorine atoms; however, salt cannot be reduced to its constituent elements because as a compound it differs from its original components. Across time and place, salt always exhibits the same consistent phenomenological properties of taste and appearance and as a compound it forms an indispensable chemical adjunct to metabolic processes in living organisms. However, salt cannot straightforwardly be decomposed back into its individual elements since its original chemical constituents – in the form of the elements sodium and chlorine – behave quite differently. In other words, the whole is different from the sum of its parts.

Perhaps, since it refers specifically to the behaviour of complex sounds which might or might not be considered musical, Fourier's theorem[52] acts as a more appropriate analogy. Simply stated, 'Any arbitrary waveform can be expressed as a sum (possibly of an infinite number) of sine waves of harmonically related frequencies' (Crecraft & Gergely 2002:23). By this theorem complex waves are conceived as built up from individual sine and cosine waves with different degrees of amplitude and phase. It follows that the constituents and the result are not identical phenomena. Hence by analogy, the musical properties (pitch, amplitude, and timbral content) which constitute a given melodic phrase are not by themselves sufficient to constitute the given phrase (for this is surely

---

[52] See Goldsmith (2015: 31–33) for a detailed explanation.

reductionist), nor do the individual members of an ensemble straightforwardly constitute 'the group.'

## 3.2 'It's about Time': the Dynamics of Dynamic Systems Theory

Arising in the early 1990s (Beer 2008), dynamic systems theory (DST) caters for changes to a given system over time. When considering musical ensembles as cases of systems, DST presents an alternative approach to laboratory-based studies of individual perception, which doubtless have yielded valuable findings for music cognition and perception, but which remove the performer from her environment and place the emphasis on individual – as opposed to group – dynamics and learning. Dynamic systems theory departs from the traditional reductionist techniques of scientific method to examine the properties and behaviour of the system as a whole as well as the actions of the individual agents constituting the system.[53] McIntyre's discussion of creativity illuminates this paradox, where the focus lies not in the brain, nor isolated patterns of thought, nor within society or culture at large, but in the inter-relationships between creative processes at a systemic level:

> [T]here is little point in looking solely at the actions or structures of the brain alone, for example, and hoping to find the reason for creativity there. Similarly, one couldn't also investigate types of thinking patterns in isolation from other factors and hope to give a definitive account of creativity by researching these alone. In the same way just concentrating on societal or cultural structures by themselves would not give complete access to what is happening in a creative act. What we need to do is include all of these processes as part of a system in operation. (McIntyre 2013: 91)

Systems theory takes account of different levels of analysis, so interrogating the differences between individual and collective intelligence. The notion of collective intelligence as emergent from individual interactions now forms a central nucleus around which varieties of practice-led and -based research (PAR) have recently begun to coalesce. This is not, strictly speaking, the same as the cases of distributed cognition described by Hutchins (1995, 2005), because all participants are immediately available (visible, audible) and hence feedback is instantaneous, in the moment.

Systems theory as applied to musical performance considers transformations of musical material over time as dynamic emergent processes constrained by the specific rituals and stylistic conventions of the environment in question. In

---

[53] This paradox speaks to a practical problem in assessing musical ensembles for examination purposes. At which level should one focus one's attention: on the activities and contributions of the individuals or the group or both? (Duby 2020).

a sense, then, all music (understood as lived experience of musical events whether from the perspective of performer, listener, dancer, singer, stage manager, or sound engineer)[54] is emergent since it changes from moment to moment. From duos to orchestras, the complex cognitive demands of ensembles provide rich and ecologically valid data (Brown, Zatorre, & Penhune 2015; Altenmüller et al. 2018) for studying cognising as real-time emergent processes.

In addition to wide ranges of complexity and sheer size, systems exhibit various operational time-scales over which they unfold. These traverse a spectrum of possibilities from the light years of galaxies to the virtual instantaneity of events at subatomic level. On a more human scale, live musical performances may last from minutes to hours, rarely days. Understanding the considerable cognitive demands of musical performance in systems thinking terms yields at least two conceptions of time: one at individual level, where the activity of practising over time transforms the plasticity of the performer's brain as well as the other, the real-time unfolding of time in and through performance.

Completely improvised music (so-called free music) stands at one end of a spectrum occupied at the other by the relative fixity of notated music such as Western art music, for instance. In the case of a symphony orchestra, the conductor acts as a limiting factor – defined by Meadows (2008: 266) as 'a necessary system input that is the one limiting the activity of the system at a particular moment' – in establishing when and how the music is to be played.

Such constraints do not apply in the case of free music where consensus prevails for the most part. Because of the absence of limiting factors, one might understand free improvisation as close to the edge of chaos (with high degrees of freedom within the system). Such a system is regarded as thermodynamically open, operating as an energy exchange system.[55]

Because of this energy flow through the system it is thereby also regarded as 'nonconservative' (Goldfield 1995: 29) and relatively susceptible to changes in phase state such that 'fluctuations can become amplified and overtake the organization of the whole system, shifting it to a new order of organization' (Thelen & Smith 2006: 269).

Ensemble performance viewed dynamically takes account of its emergence over time, howsoever such performance is constrained by various limiting factors; from a systems viewpoint, there will be points at which the ensemble

---

[54] It's tempting to assume these experiences of music are similar, but the sound engineer might be understanding 'the music' as a range of frequencies to be managed, while the dancer waits for her signal (cue) to enter from the wings, and the soloist mentally prepares for a difficult passage to come.

[55] 'Many systems, and all biological systems, live in thermodynamic nonequilibrium [and] are thermodynamically open: They take in energy from their environment and increase their order' (Thelen and Smith 2006: 269).

literally and figuratively breathes together, where collective fluctuations in tempo serve to punctuate key points in the unfolding musical narrative.

Menary (2007) maintains that these networked relationships (in this context, between instruments and performers, between performers and each other, and between performers and audiences) can be understood dynamically: 'brains, bodies and aspects of the environment can all be treated as dynamical systems, and given interactions between them, they can also be treated as parts of a single overall system – the organism–environment system' (42).

Scientists use differential equations to account for changes in the behaviour of complex systems over time. For Frankish and Ramsey (2012), proponents of DST 'contend that coordinated interactions between the world and an agent can best be explained by identifying a small number of critical variables and capturing their evolving relation over time in differential equations' (24–25). Such associations may be linear, as in a simple calculation of cost increase of a commodity over time, or non-linear whereby 'instead of one-to-one associations, values on one variable may be associated with uneven values in another' (Richardson 2010: 23).

What constitutes the dynamic element in DST is the spatio-temporal aspect and how these associations become (23) 'vastly richer structures, just as those in dancing figures and waterfalls are far more interesting than static snapshots of them'. Underlying Richardson's description is the idea of movement, whether of a natural or social phenomenon. For Gibson and ecological psychology in general, the organism *moves* as a sense-making activity to discover the affordances of the environment (see also Sheets-Johnstone 2011). Since musical performance involves highly skilled movement, it follows that the techniques and models of DST are applicable to research in that field, as they may well be for other coordinated human cultural performance activities such as dance, theatre, and sport.

## 4 The Phenomenological Turn

Heidegger famously distinguished between notions of things as 'ready-to-hand' (*Zuhanden*) or 'present-at-hand' (*Vorhanden*).[56] How – and how much – direct attention the player devotes to their chosen instrument is fundamental to distinguishing between experts and novices. Over many years as a student

---

[56] McAuliffe and Malpas (2022: 167) distinguish these ideas on the basis of relative attention; *Zuhanden* is taken to mean using a thing without direct thought, while *Vorhanden* implies direct attention focused on the thing in question. By comparison, Tanaka and Donnarumma (2018: 80) regard *Vorhanden* as tied to learning a musical instrument, whereas mastery (confident execution) corresponds with *Zuhanden*.

ensemble director, I observed Heidegger's distinction playing out countless times when some distracting element manifested itself in live performance. For example, a novice guitarist, unsettled by a colleague's unexpected departure from the formal roadmap, more often than not fixes their gaze on their own instrument, perhaps for reassurance (Duby 2022b). More seasoned musicians, on the other hand, seem to look at their instruments less often and are better equipped to watch and interact with their conspecifics as the performance unfolds.

When equipment malfunctions (a string breaks, a cable hums unexpectedly, or an amplifier breaks down), the player's attention naturally enough changes focus to attend to the immediate problem. What was ready-to-hand under the fingers can no longer be taken for granted; the necessity of solving an immediate technical problem becomes paramount.

Phenomenology places the accent on the lived experience of individuals and groups (invoking the idea of intersubjectivity). Merleau-Ponty especially emphasised that knowledge is a form of skilled activity within what he termed the 'intentional arc'[57] of daily life. Once again, this knowledge is embodied *tout court*, whether it be typing, riding a bicycle, or playing a musical instrument. For Merleau-Ponty, it is based in action itself, not in mental representations[58] which purportedly drive action. In what follows, I discuss aspects of musical 'lived experience' and how such experience might transform itself over time: in other words, musical learning.

With regard to musical meaning, Clifton[59] argues, '[W]hile it is true that a sonata by Mozart exists independently of me, it has significance *for* me to the extent that I perceive it adequately. More radically, one must say that musical meaning exists only *for* a subject who knows and judges it' (1983: 41, original emphasis). So saying, Clifton dispels the idea that musical *meaning* can exist independently of those who deal in its currency, so to speak: musicians, composers, listeners, Small's networks of participants, all are caught up in the flow of emergent and co-created musical meaning as it unfolds.

---

[57] As defined by Dreyfus (cited in Selinger and Crease 2002: 271, original emphases), 'The *intentional arc* names the tight connection between the agent and world, namely that, as the agent acquires skills, those skills are "stored", not as representations in the mind, but as dispositions to respond to the solicitations of the world.'

[58] For Zahidi (2013: 4), classical cognitive science regards 'the hallmark of true cognitive functioning [as] the building and manipulation of inner or mental representations.' His alternative approach (NRCS: non-representational cognitive science) is intended 'to develop an account of cognition without relying on internal representations' (6ff.).

[59] Clifton's (1983) *Music as Heard* represents one of the earliest systematic applications of phenomenological insight to musical experience, in the form of what he terms 'applied phenomenology'.

For Clifton (1983), 'what counts as lived musical experiences are such intuited essences as the grace of a minuet by Mozart, the drama of a symphony by Mahler, or the agony of Coltrane's jazz. If we hear the music at all, it is because we hear the grace, the drama, and the agony as essential constituents of, and irreducibly given in, the music itself' (19). The fact that we hear such qualities in the music as it unfolds does not imply that Mozart had to be in a state of grace – or Coltrane in agony, for that matter – to communicate such qualities, so sidestepping the potential absurdities of the intentional fallacy.

To grasp such 'intuited essences', then, is to understand phenomenology as a technique as much as a broad philosophical orientation. Husserl's technique of 'bracketing'[60] lays out a rigorous methodological approach for describing lived experience, what he calls 'empirical intuition'.[61] Bracketing is somewhat akin to the neologism *ostranenie*,[62] a term used by Russian Formalists to mean 'making strange' and 'pushing aside'.

In my own practice, this relates to an attempt to unsettle my own habits, such as assuming that a musical instrument is inactive, an inert 'thing' on which I impose my musical will. Here I have in mind Hayles' (2017) understanding that 'part of the contemporary turn toward the nonhuman is the realization that an object need not be alive or conscious in order to function as a cognitive agent' (212). While clearly a musical instrument is part and parcel of material culture, *it also transforms my musical understanding through my interactions with it*: hence, equally a subject or agent in a process of mutual transformation.

O'Callaghan (2012) raises objections to the accuracy of phenomenological reports, making the point that such methods as 'making strange' do not eliminate the potential influence of bias based on past experience. Consequently, for him, the claims of successful introspection are less than certain:

> Responses based on phenomenological reflection should be treated as a kind of performance that might be attributed to a variety of factors apart from accurately reporting perceptual experiences. If reports might be infused with information from other sources, such as one's background beliefs concerning the items in a scene, or some strategy adopted to respond to ambiguous

---

[60] The transcendental reduction, defined by Bowman (1998) as 'a temporary abstention from judgment in order to allow total attention to the objects and processes of consciousness as they exist in and of themselves' (257). See also Hintikka (2006).

[61] Husserl states it thus: 'Empirical intuition or, specifically, experience, is consciousness of an individual object; and as an intuitive consciousness it "makes this object given", as perception it makes an individual object given originally in the consciousness of seizing upon this object "originally", in its "personal" selfhood' (cited in Hintikka 2006: 84).

[62] www.oxfordreference.com/display/10.1093/oi/authority.20110803100256378; jsessionid=8824372BB8520A01B0279D3DA28C7D38, accessed 1 July 2023.

experiences, then perhaps no unique, epistemically privileged level of intro-spectively accessible phenomenology exists. (88)

Certainly, the warrant of this kind of phenomenological inquiry as trying to establish some 'unique, epistemically privileged level' has limits as compared to experimental data gathered in laboratories, for argument's sake. In this regard, Van Manen (2023) captures the deep, almost inexpressible connection between phenomenology and real-life practice, so placing the emphasis on the practical virtues of the phenomenological attitude:

> [P]henomenology of practice is sensitive to the realization that life as we live and experience it is not only rational and logical, and thus transparent to systematic reflection – it is also subtle, enigmatic, contradictory, ambiguous, sometimes mysterious, and saturated with existential and transcendent mean-ing that can only be accessed through poetic, aesthetic, and ethical languages. Phenomenology is a perpetual practice, an eternal practicing to get, explore, and disclose meaning in all its complexity. (4)

In short, practice is to life as life is to practice.[63] Ferrone and Gallese (2023) argue that what they term 'the bodily self' can 'provide us with the roots for self-awareness, for the sense of being in the world and acting upon it' (524). This sense of self, they maintain, is intersubjective and intercorporeal, 'as we are always already embedded in a world of social relations' (524). The next step for them (527ff.) is to develop the notion of a 'social bodily self', which enables and establishes connections to other selves by way of embodied simulation through the operations of mirror mechanisms. Neurons activated in individuals' interactions with objects also discharge, albeit more weakly, in an observer witnessing these interactions.

## 5 The Turn to Affordances

Clarke (2005) represents the first concerted attempt to bring psychology and music perception together under the aegis of ecological psychology.[64] A decade later, Tan's (2015) review lauds the 'ingenuity' and 'enduring relevance' of Clarke's project, which paved the way for scholars to apply Gibson's ideas to music perception. Most significantly, Tan notes that Clarke's focus on 'how it is that listeners *perceive* musical meaning' (original emphasis) suggests an engagement grounded in listening to music from the perspective of

---

[63] Van Manen (4) notes how 'phenomenology is primarily a philosophic method, attitude, and way of thinking and seeing,' with practical applications to professional situations as well as everyday life.

[64] 'Ecological psychology is an analytical framework that seeks to reveal lawful, functional relations in the ongoing reciprocal interaction of the individual and the environment' (Heft 2001: 6, n2).

embodiment. As Clarke (2005) states it, this environment is 'highly structured' and 'subject to both the forces of nature . . . and the profound impact of human beings and their cultures; and that in reciprocal fashion, perceivers are highly structured organisms that are adapted to their environment' (17).

On this view, the notion of the listener as part of a brain-body-environment system (and the attendant reciprocal interactions that take place between its constituents) departs from ideas of the music as 'out there' and the listener as passive consumer. This system is understood holistically, with the three elements in an intimate and inseparable relationship of mutual influence, and forms the centrepiece of ecological psychology, whence comes the idea of affordances (Chemero 2003; Dokic 2010), later applied to musicking and what it affords (Clarke 2005; Windsor 2011; Windsor and de Bezenac 2012).

It is noteworthy at the outset that Gibson largely focused his attention on visual perception,[65] placing the accent on agents moving and actively engaging with the invariant properties of their environment. Shapiro (2019) defines Gibson's term 'invariant' as 'features of the ambient optic array that remain constant under transformation'. (37) Similarly, Clarke (2005) defines a musical invariant as 'a pattern of temporal proportions and pitch intervals that is left intact, and hence retains its identity, under transformations such as pitch transposition and changes in global tempo' (35). While Clarke is referring to how the listener perceives invariants, this aspect is evident in stringed instruments where the performer can transpose a phrase to a different key by shifting the starting position and replicating the fingering.

Gibson's definition (2015: 119–135) of affordances[66] leaves much open. With regard to musical performance, this notion of affordances forms a bare-bones framework for describing the various interfaces (literally, keys, valves, strings, and so on) through which musicians engage with musical instruments. If a staircase affords 'climbability', in the sense that 'affordances provide opportunities for action' (Bardone 2010: 139)[67], one might then minimally define *musical* affordances in terms of an instrument's 'playability', so that the ongoing interactions between the clarinettist and her instrument delineate one spatio-temporal aspect of these affordances.

By invoking musical affordances with regard to the embodied listener, Clarke extends this minimal framework of musical interactions to encompass the

---

[65] See Shapiro (2019: 34–47) for an extended discussion of visual perception understood ecologically: 'The inputs to vision are various invariant features of structured light, and these features can be relied on to specify unambiguously their sources' (35).

[66] 'The *affordances* of the environment are what it *offers* the animal, what it *provides* or *furnishes*, either for good or ill' (Gibson 2015: 119, original emphases).

[67] Consider, though, that the affordances of a staircase vary in the case of neonates and elderly persons, suggesting that 'climbability' is a variable action possibility, not an ecological fact.

broader social structures that enable listening as a sense-making activity (see also Schiavio & De Jaegher 2017). Again, noting the open quality of Gibson's original definition, this move is justified, so that the broad notion of affordances in music is not incongruent with Gibson's claims. However, it's worth a reminder that Gibson originally dealt with visual perception[68] and treated notions of affordances and resonances as part of the direct realism project.

In this regard, Bardone (2010) sounds an appropriately cautious note in saying: 'Becoming attuned to invariants and disturbances often goes beyond the mere Gibsonian direct perception and higher representational[69] and mental processes of thinking/learning have to be involved' (142). Well, yes and no, depending on the complexity of the organism in question and how one defines mental processes. We have already seen how Maturana et al. extended cognition to organisms without nervous systems, so that their understanding of cognition includes all manner of earthly creatures. By implication, affordances are not limited to human interactions and Bardone's example of a door's affordances must surely depend, like the staircase, on the creature's own capabilities to realise the door's affordances as *effective* possibilities for action.[70]

Heras-Escribano (2019) notes how in some instances the concept of affordances has been taken out of its original context in ecological psychology. The consequences of this move are that 'The notion has been stripped away from its original context and adapted to other contexts, theories, and approaches, which means that its full potential has not been yet displayed and that its meaning is confused with other elements that have nothing to do with affordances' (4). To try to head off these objections, I am therefore proffering a 'minimal' interpretation of musical affordances with its point of origin the interactions between musician and instrument.

From Maturana's all-encompassing understanding of cognition, it follows that not all creatures understand affordances in the same way as human beings do. Recall that Gibson's notion of affordances claims that the environment offers *a range of possibilities for action and interaction*. One might then ask what kinds of thought processes a simple organism might deploy in assessing

---

[68] Gibson understands visual perception as part of a *perceptual system*, in which are intertwined the perceiving creature and its environment. Penny (2017: 28) writes that 'Gibson's notion of perceptual systems is a dynamical and embodied conception that emphasizes the role of the individual's self-directed movements in revealing environmental structure. This makes vision in Gibson's terms embodied and proprioceptively integrated.'

[69] 'The explanatory work that is supposedly done by mental representations, can however instead be done by looking outside of the head to the environment structured by sociomaterial practices, and the affordances it makes available' (Kiverstein & Rietveld 2020: n.p.).

[70] It seems only fair to acknowledge that Bardone is aware of this aspect when he states that 'The same event or place can provide different affordances to different organisms but also multiple affordances to the same organism' (Bardone 2010).

the affordances of a waterhole, for instance, beyond the immediate biological imperative of quenching thirst. This scenario seems to speak to a more limited view of affordances based on direct perception.

Bardone (2010: 143) casts the 'traditional view' of affordances in these terms: 'The traditional view on affordance considers direct perception as prerequisite to an affordance. To put it simply, if we do not have direct perception, then we do not have an affordance. If this were correct, then the contribution of affordance for distributed cognition theory would be poor.' If we take this caveat seriously, it points to a need for more caution in extending Gibson's notion of affordances beyond its original – admittedly broad – remit.[71] It remains for the reader to decide whether or not extending affordances in such a way does justice to his original, somewhat modest, claims. Put another way, is Gibson's dependence on direct realism (and the useful framework of affordances) compatible with enactive cognition? I will attend to this problem in the conclusion of this Element.

When Rietveld (2008) describes in phenomenological terms the 'affective allure' and possibilities of potentiation offered by affordances (977), this brings to mind the complex relationship over time that has developed between humans and musical instruments, with archaeological evidence marking the origin of musical instruments from between thirty-six and forty thousand years ago. Cross and Morley (2010: 74ff.) speak of 'a marked increase in the evidence for musical activities' from around thirty thousand years ago, including fossil evidence and exploitation of the acoustic properties of specific environments (such as rocks and caves). These writers suggest that, despite a paucity of confirming evidence, our musician ancestors seem to have preferred performing in groups: 'These musical activities seem to have been widespread, often occurring in what appear to be loci of intense human activity, which includes the making of graphical art. The evidence – fragmentary as it is – suggests that musical performance was a group activity, rather than one involving a select few individuals' (74).

Reading affordances 'as an organism's possibilities for action in some situation', Rietveld's (2008) inquiry is concerned with developing 'a better understanding of the way skilled individuals are responsive to relevant affordances while engaged in a flow of actions. Part of the first-person experience of such responsiveness is that affordances are not mere possibilities for action but are experienced as potentiating and having affective allure' (976–977). His remarks on skilled engagement seem especially appropriate since the relationships

---

[71] Also see Segundo-Ortin and Heras-Escribano (2023) for a rejection of ideas of 'mental' and 'cognitive' affordances.

musicians form with their instrument of choice[72] and the cognitive demands of high-level musical performance exemplify the possibilities for agency these tools of the trade afford. As for their allure, this potential represents the billion-dollar musical instrument manufacturing industry; according to Fortune Business Insights.com:[73] 'The global musical instrument market size was valued at USD 18.63 billion in 2022 and is projected to grow from USD 19.25 billion in 2023 to USD 24.53 billion by 2030, exhibiting a CAGR of 3.52% during the forecast period.'

The complex bundle of skills demonstrated by the expert performer encompasses memorising, expressive nuanced improvisation, precise dexterity, and speed of movement, as Zatorre and her colleagues argue in the case of Dave Brubeck:

> When he performed his standard 'The Duke' in a televised or live performance, he was demonstrating one of the most demanding cognitive and motor behaviors of which humans are capable. Audiences marveled at his ability to perform a long and complex piece of music entirely from memory. Listeners were also astounded by his ability to bring the piece to life by embellishing, improvising, and continuously changing the expressive nuances of his performance. Audiences were equally amazed at the speed, dexterity, and precision of his movements on the piano. (Brown, Zatorre, & Penhune 2015: 57–58)

While this vivid description certainly succeeds in underlining the cognitive demands of expert musical performance, it is worth noting that Brubeck generally played with an ensemble, as opposed to Keith Jarrett, for instance, who has developed a solo career (Thompson & Ammirante 2012) in parallel with his ensemble projects. Coordinating ensemble performance requires additional gestural, communication, and interaction skills, not to mention those involving leadership and management capabilities.

With regard to affordances in the cases of Brubeck and Jarrett, these do not mysteriously reside inside the piano itself, but rather in the interface between

---

[72] An important systems-theoretical aspect of Instrument–performer relationships can be described by deploying the concept of feedback. Through her senses of hearing, sight, and touch, the musician's actions set in motion auditory phenomena which provide information for the self-regulation of intonation and other musical properties such as sense of musical time, control of volume and timbral characteristics, and synchronisation with other performers, among others. The individual feedback loop between instrument and performer is thus nested within another feedback loop at ensemble level. In turn, the ensemble loop in live performance situations more often than not involves a further feedback system incorporating the audience's interactive responses to the music as it unfolds. Thompson and Ammirante (2012: 774) similarly claim that musicians 'perform differently depending on the perceived attitude and energy of their listeners.'

[73] Available at https://www.fortunebusinessinsights.com/musical-instrument-market-108706.

musician and instrument. These in turn play out in a reciprocal relationship that develops over a long period of preparation and acquaintanceship to develop the core action-perception, haptic – by way of Gibson's concept of 'dynamic touch'[74] – (Michaels, Weier, & Harrison 2007), motor, and auditory discrimination skills that are manifested apparently without effort in expert performances.

As expertise grows over time, the performer accumulates a store of tacit embodied knowledge[75] (the knowledge of how to make the right moves) and begins more and more to offload in-the-moment skills such as dexterity to subliminal memory. While not intending to erase the nuances of difference between these approaches, this notion of embodied knowledge lies at the heart of the shared concerns of ecological psychology and the phenomenological project, what Heft (2007) describes as 'the central tenet of ecological psychology: organism-environment reciprocity' (88).

From a systems perspective, the technological refinements over time as musical instruments have evolved – and continue to do so (see Barclay 2011 for a historical overview) – point to a similar musical evolution on two fronts: ontogenetically for individuals over the course of a performing career and phylogenetically as the gradual accumulation of a store of common cultural knowledge. As Heft (2001) argues in this regard:

> One particularly important feature of artifacts, symbolic representations, and social structures is that knowledge acquired by individuals and collectively by social groups can be 'off-loaded' onto them. In so doing, the amount of knowledge that can be retained over time increases enormously, and the accumulation and refinement of knowledge through iterations across generations becomes possible. These innovations, in effect, create possibilities for knowledge to become distributed across the environment-person(s) relation, considered at varying levels of complexity. (385)

Applying this thinking to the operations of a symphony orchestra yields the example of symbolic representations such as notated music – a mnemonic device demanding high levels of individual sight-reading ability and instrumental competence – but also social skills such as being a good ensemble player, and responsiveness to gestural and auditory cues in the musical realisation of the conductor's directions. It follows from this that there exists not only embodied

---

[74] The emphasis on Gibson's ideas of visual perception in the literature neglects his admittedly more circumscribed discussions of touch and haptic systems. Generally, these perceptual systems are treated more or less in isolation and Gibson places the most emphasis on vision. Gibson very rarely, if ever, mentions music as a field of inquiry, hence Clarke's application of ecological psychology to musical practice remains an innovative strategy.

[75] What Hayles (2017) calls 'the cognitive nonconscious'.

sensorimotor knowledge (knowing how to realise a complex musical phrase) but also knowledge of one's roles and limits (in systems terms, behavioural constraints) within an ensemble setting.

This type of social intelligence may be intuitive or managed by a section leader in an orchestra as part of an often-unstated master/apprentice relationship but in either case it contributes to an understanding of how to behave appropriately in the course of performance. Kelso's (2003) concept of coordination dynamics goes beyond the individualistic rationality of cognitivism to take account of the irreducible complexity of human action:

> Self-organizing dynamics tends to emphasize decentralization, collective decision-making, and cooperative behavior among many interacting elements. Conventional cognitive psychology tends to focus on individual psychological processes such as intention, perception, attention, memory, action, and so on, as if they were clearly isolable. Yet, as evidence and theory now show, intending, perceiving, attending, deciding and remembering – as well as spontaneous self-organizing aspects – are essential, coexisting attributes of cognitive coordination dynamics. (62)

These attributes relate closely to a description of distributed cognition during heart surgery as proffered by Semin and colleagues (Semin, Garrido, & Palma 2012: 153):

> What the team shares is knowledge about the joint activity and the coordination of these activities. Thus, the specialized knowledge that each individual holds is crucial for the performance of the task, and this knowledge is distributed across the individual members of the team. The coordinated product of the individuals constitutes a type of collectively constituted knowledge or cognition that is unique because the entire process of the operation is not a single person's production but a collectively coordinated 'cognition as action' that drives the operation from its beginning to its end.

Hence the operations of such teams – like the analogies with household salt and Fourier's theorem (3.1) – are not decomposable into the actions of individuals. In the literature, the phenomenon of collective knowledge that drives group activities goes by any number of names: cognitive coordination dynamics (Kelso 2003), distributed cognition (Hutchins 1995, 2005), collective intelligence (Malone & Bernstein 2015), and group dynamics (Arrow, McGrath, & Berdahl 2000; Agazarian & Gantt 2005; McIntyre 2013).

Despite their theoretical differences, such approaches share the understanding that cognising does not only deal with rational processes but draws from a storehouse of individual and collective knowledge, often unverbalised because it is subliminal, in a sense prior to and different from language and consequently often hard to explain, so-called procedural knowledge.

## 6 The Turn to Practice

Malafouris (2020: 3), pointing out psychology's apparent lack of interest in 'the relation between cognition and material culture', raises this question: 'How are things (in the broadest anthropological sense of material forms, flows, and techniques) related to thinking?' To address these concerns, he proposes a theory of mutually transforming interactions between agents and artefacts (Material Engagement theory).

Practice is in time, about time, and of its time. Musical practice is about human entanglement with things (Malafouris 2013) and the nature of the times and spaces in which these play out. If music is all 'about time', whose and what kind of time is in play (pun intended)? By which model of time do we understand its processual unfolding? Notice, for instance, how ordinary language both commodifies and reifies time (making and wasting, losing and gaining time, overtime) or ties it to clock time, as in or out of time, and about time.

Musicians are concerned with musical time, naturally enough, and in the recording studio accurate time[76] is a hallmark of good musicianship. Rhythm is perceived through time. Expressed as consonant or dissonant with regard to an underlying regular pulse, implicit or obvious, rhythmic and polyrhythmic patterns emerge from the interactions of musicians in and through time.

Commenting on the 'radical novelty' of recent work investigating the body's crucial role in musical performance, Jensenius (2022) reminds us that 'musical experiences should be understood as interactions between human bodies and musical instruments' (xiii). These interactions have recently become fertile ground for exploration, with a number of new works appearing in which such interactions (and the body's role therein) take centre stage, as it were. Beginning with Clarke (2005) and Leman (2008), contributions from various quarters have sought to explore the intimate relationship between human bodies and musicking practices. Examples include LeSaffre et al. (2017), de Souza (2017), Cobussen (2017), Hoppe and Müller (2021), Reybrouck (2021), Jensenius (2022), van der Schyff et al. (2022), and a locally edited volume on embodiment and the arts (Lauwrens 2022)[77].

---

[76] The Russian Dragon was devised to monitor exactly how accurately musicians enact musical time: www.soundonsound.com/reviews/jeanius-electronics-russian-dragon-rd-r3, accessed 28 March 2024.

[77] In introducing the aims and objectives of the book, Lauwrens (2022: 8) argues that 'embodiment acknowledges both the material body and the body's orientation in the environment – physically, psychically, emotionally, cognitively and intellectually. This spatial or environmental dimension of embodiment includes one's actions, moods, perceptions, personal experiences and the cultural contexts and personalities that shape them.'

The purpose of this section is to consider how various notions of interactions play out in the context of my own musical experience as a multi-instrumentalist. Against the backdrop of embodied musicking, I explore the grain of my own musical experience as related to musical knowledge from a first-person perspective, mediated through my chosen instruments: the double bass, the bass guitar, and the electric guitar.

Schiavio et al. (2023: 534) define extended musical historicity as 'the complex interplay of felt, imagined and predicted shared experiences by which each musical agent relates to a broader (past, present or future) social ecology'. They acknowledge the role of communities of practice[78] (Wenger 1998; Lave 1991; Lave 2008) within which individuals and groups enact various forms of musical behaviour which develop over time, concluding that 'even in solitary musical activity, rich, multi-levelled histories of social participation underwrite every set of actions and, to varying degrees, guide the meaningful experiences that arise in a given musical situation'.[79] While the descriptions of my own musical practice in what follows mostly refer to my experiences as an individual practitioner, I recognise that even in the relative isolation of my studio, such experiences are framed by sociality in a number of senses.

While clearly I am the individual person responsible for initiating physical action to create musical sounds, even in solitude I am 'plugged in'[80] to my own community of practice, whether real or imagined. Through my own idiosyncratic musical history, I have engaged with a range of musical canons through looking back on – and listening to – archival recordings and performances on DVDs, playing along with these, experiencing live concerts in the moment as spectator and participant, perusing scores, and so on. In this way, my personal musical historicity extends to the past, is enacted in the present moment through the embodied actions of performance, and looks to the future in refining musical skills over time.

In so doing, I am engaging in what Dieleman (2012) defines as 'reflexive action'. He insists on the irreducibility and inseparability of knowledge and skills as constituents of this type of action. Following Schön's work on practice,

---

[78] 'There are highly valued forms of knowledgeable skill in this society for which learning is structured in apprentice-like forms. Furthermore, once one begins to think in terms of legitimate peripheral participation in communities of practice, many other forms of socially organized activity become salient' (Lave 1991: 64–65).

[79] They continue: 'That said, there are, of course, important phenomenological differences between solitary situations and those in which others are physically co-present. Likewise, although the meanings and uses of a tool (a computer, a musical instrument and so on) emerge from a history of practice involving others, this is not the same as the joint sense of agency that is experienced when two or more people use that tool to realize a shared goal' (542).

[80] This turn of phrase is intended to hark back to 'plug-ins', computer-based digital simulations of analogue equipment.

Dieleman defines reflexive action (49) as 'a sequence of actions to achieve a goal and when we know well how to do it, we have difficulty in saying how we did it'. This definition gets to the heart of the tension between procedural knowledge ('knowhow': for him, driving, playing a musical instrument, and sports such as basketball and tennis) and its translation into speech or writing for communicative purposes as declarative knowledge. Dieleman (49) understands reflexive action in transdisciplinary fashion as 'an integration of experiences, skills and knowledge in action within an integrated system'. In a feedback loop, experience affects knowledge and emotions, which in turn affect the experience in question.

## 6.1 The First-Person Perspective

Froese (Froese 2012: 144) argues for the necessity of a first-person perspective as a counterweight to the purported objectivity of the scientific approach.[81] If scientific certainty is the driving force, we must either surrender our first-person perspective as embodied agents or abandon notions of scientific objectivity. This hardly seems a fair choice since it draws a rigid disciplinary boundary between first-person experience and the tenets of objectivity[82] which scientific inquiry demands. The consequences of the quest for objectivity are the exile of subjective knowledge to what Nicolescu (2010: 19) terms 'the inferno of subjectivity, tolerated at most as a meaningless embellishment or rejected with contempt as a fantasy, an illusion, a regression, or a product of the imagination'.

Whether or not these demands are mutually exclusive remains subject to debate, but recent developments in practice-led, practice-based, and cognate research agendas connected to various forms of artistic practice seem to prove otherwise. Such agendas strive to provide subjective but rigorous accounts of practice as process, placing the emphasis more on processes as they unfold than the outcome of the activity. As Metzinger states it (cited in Wittmann 2016: 103): 'the self is not so much a thing as a process'.

---

[81] I am well aware that this convenient shorthand does not do justice to the wide variety of scientific methods appropriate to the researchers' chosen fields. What is at stake is less the particular methodology than the necessity of objectivity in legitimising scientific inquiry. For Nicolescu (2010: 19): 'Modern science was ... founded on the idea – surprising and revolutionary for that era – of a total separation between the knowing subject and Reality, which was assumed to be completely independent from the subject who observed it.'

[82] 'The basic claim of science is objectivity: it attempts, through the application of a well-defined methodology, to make statements about the universe. At the very root of this claim, however, lies its weakness: the *a priori* assumption that objective knowledge constitutes a description of what is known' (Maturana & Varela 1980: 5). Recall that second-order cybernetics includes the observer's subjective situation.

While I am in broad sympathy with this claim regarding selfhood as a state of perpetual becoming as opposed to a spatio-temporal body-object, Metzinger grounds the notion of subjective experience in 'complex patterns of neural activation in the brain' (103). These undoubtedly complex brain-based patterns operate on a different stratum from a creaturely body moving in time and space, which draws in other embodied interactive networks[83] for survival, and brain-based patterns alone surely cannot fully account for the necessary adaptation to circumstances evident in spatio-temporal presence and related activities. The organism's survival cannot depend solely on skull-based activity but for purposes of ecological validity must be considered as a complex, dynamic, and moving whole.[84]

The life of the mind[85] implies a subject: a human being whose subjectivity cannot merely be swept aside in the interests of scientific objectivity: an agent, a person with all the richness and complexity that personhood carries with it. The scientific search for objective certainty, when it disregards human agency, is incongruent with the sense of self Wittmann (2016) describes in stating that: 'The feeling of an enduring self with a personal history and the capacity to influence the future defines us as persons' (51). Understanding personhood as a dynamic unfolding process allows for the subjectivity of aliveness and what Fuchs (2011) calls 'a unity of interiority and exteriority':

> What is lost in the principal divide is the human person which essentially means *a living being*, an embodied subject. The person is neither pure subjectivity experienced from within, nor a complex physiological system observed from without; it is a living being interacting with others from a second-person or 'you'-perspective, and thus, as a unity of interiority and exteriority. When talking with another person, listening to his words, seeing him laughing, shaking hands with him, etc. we perceive him both as a conscious, experiencing being and as a physical, bodily being at the same · time. (198–199)

Fuchs (2021) invokes Merleau-Ponty's notion of intercorporeality as a basis for understanding how human beings learn to empathise through physical

---

[83] For example, Penny (2017) points out how 'The enteric nervous system (ENS), sometimes referred to as a second brain, contains around one hundred million neurons – three orders of magnitude less than the brain, to be sure, but not an insubstantial number' (36).

[84] See Sheets-Johnstone (2011: 478–489) for a discussion of the dynamic nature of mind. She writes: 'In effect, mind is not a solid and is not reducible to something solid, i.e. to *the brain*' (482, original emphasis). Referring to Metzinger, the ego is not *reducible* to skull-bound neural patterns of activation. Froese (2012) argues along the same lines in claiming that 'We all know from our own personal lives that there is more to people than what is revealed by recordings of internal physiological data and measurements of external movement patterns' (144).

[85] Or mind in life, as Thompson (2007) entitles it.

contact. His defence of the human being does not turn back to antiquated notions of the nobility of individual freedom but attempts to counter reductionist tendencies in neuroscience and the uncritical adoption of a 'scientistic' view of humanity. He highlights the use of AI in authoritarian regimes which tracks aspects of human behaviour for purposes of control so that human beings are reduced to mere agglomerations of data: computationalism run amok, if you will.

Notions of distance and objectivity are highly problematic in the performing arts. I believe that the warrant of objectivity demanded by the natural sciences, for argument's sake, does not fit something as intimate and apparently 'subjective' as musical performance. I am also wary of this claim, in so far as it may appear to reinforce the difference – and distance – between the arts and sciences that appears entrenched in contemporary academia.

## 6.2 The Creative Hand

Wilson (1999: 159) claims that '[t]ouch – the genius of the fingers – is life and death to a pianist'. Wilson's argument approaches musical skill from the outside, so to speak; he is not a musician, but a neurologist specialising in hand injuries that musicians incur in the course of pursuing their careers. He writes: 'any theory of human intelligence which ignores the interdependence of hand and brain function, the historic origins of that relationship, or the impact of that history on developmental dynamics in modern humans, is grossly misleading and sterile' (207).

The cognitive science (of Wilson's time, at least) seems to have ignored entirely the new possibilities that 'the creative hand' offers for understanding musical performance, whether neophytes or experts. However, since then, a number of scholars have offered arguments that do indeed contemplate the wide range of possibilities that the human hand offers, among them Sudnow (2001), Radman (2013), and McGinn (2015).

> So, too, with musicians. The inertia of strings, membranes, and static air columns resists the player's initial attempts to control them. This relationship, through which the player gradually negotiates and learns to manage her instrument's inherent resistance, requires time. As a result, even the most virtuosic musician must begin at the beginning, acquiring notions of heft, inertia, weight and other physical qualities (in short, instrumental affordances) through active touch, learned and mastered through action-perception cycles that encompass both feedback and feedforward networks. (Duby 2020: 8)

A musician's practice begins with hands – and, in some cases, feet[86] – whose concerted and coordinated realisation through praxis brings forth musical sound.[87] As Gallagher (2011) argues from an enactive perspective, 'Patterns of hand use physically shape those sensory and motor parts of the brain that register and control hand movement in monkeys, as well as in humans' (214). He points to the ways in which learning to play a musical instrument reconfigures the learning brain, rewiring neuronal pathways as the musician gradually builds (and refines) a storehouse of sensorimotor knowledge.

Altenmüller et al. (2018: 459) argue that the 'strong coupling of perception and action mediated by sensory, motor, and multimodal integration areas distributed throughout the brain' on which musical performance relies is explicable in terms of transformations in brain plasticity over time as professional musicians engage in 'prolonged goal-directed practice' (459). This is one example of the transformations that the demands of skilled musical performance[88] entail. Consequently, they maintain that the field of musical performance and the attendant gradual changes in brain plasticity as musicians develop higher levels of expertise provide an appropriate model for studying such changes.

> Singing and playing an instrument involve the precise execution of very fast and, in many instances, extremely complex movements that must be structured and coordinated with continuous auditory, somatosensory, and visual feedback. Furthermore, it requires retrieval of musical, motor, and multisensory information from both short-term and long-term memory and relies on continuous planning of an ongoing performance in working memory. (459)

This complex information may or may not include the interpretation of musical scores, which interpretation begins with a visual interaction with the score. As Johnson and Larson (2003) understand it, 'The score is one metaphorical representation of the imaginary path through an abstract musical space' (73). Naturally, the score may be understood as a metaphor, but it also exists as a handwritten or printed artefact, a form of shorthand for the appropriate physical movements for its realisation. Johnson and Larson argue that neither

---

[86] Here I have in mind kit drummers (Bruford 2018; Brennan et al., 2021, Smith 2021, 2022) and organists (Merleau-Ponty 2002), cases where all four limbs produce sound, as opposed to the pedals of the piano, which modify sounds produced by the hands.

[87] It's also worth noting that such praxis sometimes unfolds in less than favourable circumstances and that no outcomes are guaranteed in advance, especially when improvisation is factored into the proceedings.

[88] The complex physical and neurocognitive demands of professional performance can sometimes exceed the player's capabilities. Altenmüller and his colleagues (2018) also describe musician's dystonia in terms of 'a degradation of skilled motor behaviour' (460). See also Section 5.4.

musical scores nor the brute vibrational properties of sound (O'Callaghan 2007, 2012, 2017) can fully capture the richness of a given musical experience: 'Music is not the notes on the scores. Nor is it merely the vibrations of air that we hear as sounds. It is, rather, our whole vast rich experience of sounds synthesized by us into meaningful patterns that extend over time' (77).

This notion of 'meaningful patterns,' with its Batesonian ring, can be extended to include meaningful *movements* by performers, whose embodied interpretative actions transform symbols on a page[89] into sounding music, so bringing forth a given soundscape. Insofar as the symbols on the page do not speak for themselves, the synthesis aspect Johnson and Larson have in mind (how these patterns become meaningful, in other words) makes room for enactive sense-making as an interpretative approach.

The enactive approach suggests that perception is a limited capacity, involving the creative element of sense making to complete the circle, as it were. In this sense, musical sound exhibits 'floating intentionality'[90] (Cross 2007: 655), more ambiguous in meaning than language and understood as bound to its cultural context and function. Its situation in culture as dynamic process – which speaks to music's unfolding in and through time – allows for understanding through participation (participatory sense making for listeners and performers alike),[91] misinterpretation, misunderstanding, and in the music as it unfolds.

Musical bodies also improvise. Similarly, such content may include room for improvisation (largely exiled from the common practice period in Western art music, but alive and well in jazz and a diverse range of more or less 'traditional' musical genres). In such approaches, there is room made for musical communication which allows for the individual musician to 'tell her own story' to a degree, by playing with melody and other musical elements, in accordance with the norms of the genre in question. It seems, however, that the wide variety of genre-related improvisational practices preclude the formation of an all-encompassing 'general theory' of improvisation.

Cobussen (2017) describes the 'actors, factors, and vectors' (28) which go to make up the field of musical improvisation (FMI), eschewing such grand theory to present 'complexity and singularity' as the core elements in his FMI theory (43). He defines complexity as 'the dynamic, non-linear, and constantly changing interactions between several (independent) actors and factors that lead to

---

[89] Privileging musical scores or notational systems in general excludes the vast majority of musicians who perform without them. This begs the question of what representational resources, if any, such musicians need to realise their musical goals.

[90] Cross (2007: 655) suggests that 'the meanings of any particular musical act or event are susceptible to different, and perhaps even conflicting, interpretations, by participants'.

[91] Listeners and performers experience music from different vantage points, so (once again) the grain of these experiences may very well differ from individual to individual.

**Figure 1** 'The solid geometry of things is best got by feeling them' (Gibson 1962: 484). The author in a recording session (2018). By permission of Felicity van Pletzen.

various forms of self-organization' and regards improvising as evidence of 'complex systems, as systems continuously trying to find a balance (or to create a tension) between fixity and fluidity' (43).

## 6.3 The Double Bass

The double bass and its part in the rhythm section drove the North American jazz recordings I gravitated to in adolescence as the anchor for the more intricate improvisations of saxophonists, trumpeters, and pianists (Figure 1). While to me the bass guitar bespoke rock, blues, and more danceable forms, the double bass epitomised acoustic jazz. Miles Davis' *Kind of Blue* (1959) with Paul Chambers, *Mingus Ah Um* (of the same year) with Charles Mingus as composer/arranger and bassist, Dave Brubeck's *Time Out*, with 'Senator' Eugene Wright, Ornette Coleman's recordings with Charlie Haden: the improvised displays of high creativity on these recordings (to my mind and ears) were possible only because of the grounding, foundational aspect of the double bass.

Together with the drums,[92] the bass provides rhythmic and harmonic support for the soloists by unambiguously defining the roots. My early engagements with this acoustic jazz canon contained no such musical insights, but the sonority of the bass and its flexibility in the hands of such iconic musicians appealed directly to me.

In the formative years of my concert-going in Cape Town (a kind of aural apprenticeship, if you like) the double bass was a comparative rarity. Two memorable sightings (and hearings) spring most immediately to mind: Midge Pike playing one or two numbers with HAMMAK on double bass (where he used a bow and electronic accoutrements to alter the sound) and John Lockwood at the Space Theatre with Merton Barrow's Jazz Workshop.[93] I marvelled at Lockwood's playing the head of Miles Davis' *So What* on double bass as Paul Chambers had done in 1959. This immediacy of this experience was a far cry from listening to records. Lockwood's apparently effortless execution of *So What*'s opening phrases on this unwieldy instrument seemed superhuman to me at the time.

Seeing Pike and Lockwood on double bass live and listening to many jazz recordings featuring the double bass inspired me to take up the instrument (Audio 1). Unlike guitars and bass guitars, the double bass is more closely related to the violin family,[94] and the large fingerboard has no frets: relative acres of space, in which only a small span is actually in tune. Using the bow helps to refine the player's ear and sense of pitch to hone this skill. The heavy gauge strings demand stamina and strength in the hands[95]. Over time, the player develops callouses over the initial blisters, so that the effective execution of

**Audio 1** Author's composition: 'The general's losses.' Audio file available at www.cambridge.org/Duby

---

[92] In general, bassists and drummers form an indivisible unit: the rhythm section, and solo bass recordings are comparatively rare. According to Colin Larkin (2006) (*The Encyclopedia of Popular Music*), Barre Phillips's *Basse Barre* (1968–69) is credited as the first solo bass record in jazz.

[93] In an interview with Colin Miller (1998), Barrow describes his motivation in establishing the Jazz Workshop as a site for informal jazz education against the background of the Cape Town jazz scene in the 1950s and 60s. 'I wanted to have certain of my music played and a lot of people weren't reading enough. I couldn't write anything, I couldn't write to (sic) much because of there (sic) inability to read.'
This was some three decades before the establishment of formal jazz education in South Africa in the 1980s (see Duby 2016).

[94] Referring to the period 1650–1700, Barclay (2011) writes: 'The instruments of the viol family were displaced by those of the violin, with the result that few changes of any importance to this discussion were made to them. The exception was the violone, the bass of the family, which had been adopted as a continuo instrument and continued in that role. The sloping shoulders of the modern double bass, unique among the unfretted bowed strings, are an echo of that old viol tradition' (26).

[95] It seems to me that these demands must also enlist the entire musculoskeletal system, so that aspects of stamina and strength involve the player's entire body. Playing the double bass is profoundly corporeal in Legrand's sense of it (2011: 209, original emphasis): 'For the self to

*pizzicato*[96] is facilitated by practice. The double bass sounds different from its electric counterpart (the bass guitar) because of the large resonant cavity (the body) and in those early days amplification of the piezoelectric pickups of the time was problematic because of impedance mismatches with amplifiers.

## 6.4 The Bass Guitar

The bass guitar shares the $E_1$ $A_1$ $D_2$ $G_2$ configuration of the double bass and was introduced in the early 1950s as a more portable alternative to the double bass. Typified by the Fender Jazz Bass® (see Figure 2) and Precision Bass®, the design of these bread-and-butter instruments[97] has not changed substantially since the rock 'n' roll era; while manufactured from more advanced materials (especially as regards pickups), in recent times the basic twin-cutaway body shape has remained consistent. Bass guitar notation writes the notes an octave up from their sounding pitches (the same as guitar and double bass), largely to minimise the use of leger lines, which makes all of these transposing instruments.

Together with the electric guitar, the bass guitar typifies the sound of rock (Paul McCartney, Phil Lesh, Jack Bruce, John Paul Jones), Motown (James Jamerson), and funk (Larry Graham Jr),[98] and its relatively small size and capacity for amplification have made it more or less ubiquitous in contemporary

**Figure 2** 1966 Fender Jazz Bass (Th. Ott, CC BY-SA 3.0 <http://creativecom mons.org/licenses/by-sa/3.0/>, via Wikimedia Commons).

---

belong to the world, there is no other way than being corporeal. Not only being an experiencing subject, but more specifically being an experiencing *body* is necessary for there to be an experienced world at all.'

[96] Unlike orchestral music where the double bass is normally bowed, *pizzicato* is prevalent in jazz (the walking bass line) and other traditional musics (folk, bluegrass, and so on).

[97] By this, I mean the basic four-string configuration as above. Nowadays, five- and six-string variants featuring a low B (and an added high C for the six-string) are not uncommon.

[98] Ex-bassist of the funk band Sly and the Family stone, Graham is widely acknowledged as the inventor of the 'slap' style of bass-playing. This style alternates the thumb (imitating the bass drum) and index finger (the snare), together with dead notes, to produce a uniquely rhythmic and percussive effect. Other proponents of this style include Stanley Clarke, Bootsy Collins, Victor Wooten, Marcus Miller, Flea, Tony Levin, and Mark King.

**Audio 2** Author's composition: 'A blind bargain. Audio file available at
www.cambridge.org/Duby

popular music (Audio 2). Jaco Pastorius' first solo album (1976), featuring his
fretless[99] Jazz Bass™, showcases his virtuosic approach to the instrument exemplified by his use of harmonics (*Portrait of Tracy*), clean articulation of technically
demanding phrases (*Donna Lee*), and signature sound (*Continuum*). He was
among a select few bassists who staged solo concerts (*Honestly*) in which he
sometimes used a looper pedal to repeat a bassline over which he improvised an
added melodic part. Pastorius did much to bring the bass guitar to the front of the
stage in recognition of its melodic – as well as rhythmic and percussive – potential.

Once musicians grasped the advantages of the instrument (portability,
amplification, and so on), the double bass was more or less effectively supplanted
in popular music, at least, by the bass guitar. Once the impedance mismatch
problems posed by piezoelectric pickups for double bass were addressed, it was
not long before various hybrid solid-body electric double basses appeared on the
scene. The German bassist/composer Eberhard Weber uses such a hybrid
instrument (also known as an electric upright bass or EUB), a five-string variant
with an added high C string (1993).

Weber's composition *Sand-Glass* (from *Yellow Fields*)[100] opens with an
E Lydian *pizzicato* ostinato, soon joined by an ascending bowed accompanying
line. Both the bass and Rainer Brüninghaus' electric piano and synthesizer are
electronically processed (mainly using chorus effects) in a soundscape that
typifies the sound world of fusion, rather than mainstream jazz.

Following a stroke in 2007 which left him unable to play the bass, Weber has
released solo recordings[101] featuring the distinctive sonority of his EUB at the
forefront.

---

[99] In general, unfretted bass instruments exhibit a slightly slower attack than their fretted counterparts.
The fingers' point of direct contact with the strings and fingerboard produces a different onset
character.

[100] 'Impressionistic in intent, Weber's music emphasized mood and atmosphere above the
dexterity of the players, or as he put it to *Impetus* magazine, "I'm more interested in teamwork and the total sound, rather than the individual sounds." He was also at pains, in this
period, to emphasize his distance from the jazz tradition, preferring to feature Charlie
Mariano (whose credits include work with Mingus, McCoy Tyner, Elvin Jones) on soprano –
"the horn that has the least specific 'jazz' associations" – and the Indian nagaswaram and
shenai, rather than on his more habitual alto sax.' https://ecmrecords.com/product/yellow-
fields-eberhard-weber/, accessed 26 June 2023.

[101] *Résumé* (2012) and *Encore* (2015) are recorded compilations of his solos with keyboard
overdubs by Weber and additional material by Jan Garbarek, Ack van Rooyen, and Michael
di Pasqua.

## 6.5 The Electric Guitar

I began playing acoustic guitar quite early in my musical journey (in the early to middle 1960s). Beatlemania was all the rage at the time, with the release of Sgt Pepper's in 1967 a major milestone in my musical development. The album looked and sounded different from their previous offerings and the opening hard-edged guitar riff of the title track portended a more aggressive approach. The subject matter had moved on from romantic topics of adolescence (broadly speaking) to hitherto taboo topics like drug use ('Lucy in the sky with diamonds', 'A day in the life'), putative sexual encounters with authority figures ('Lovely Rita meter maid'), and domestic abuse ('Fixing a hole'); heady material indeed for my eleven-year-old self.[102]

Psychedelia was in the air. The LSD-inspired colours and artwork of Cream's (1968) *Wheels of Fire* confirmed that things weren't what they used to be. Eric Clapton's and Jack Bruce's distorted tone on guitar and bass respectively bespoke large amplifiers cranked to their limits, rampant energy, and high volume (especially on the live half of this double album). But it was Jimi Hendrix who truly embodied revolution. His hip lyrics and singing, instrumental virtuosity, and the raw energy of his muscular riffing elicited hero-worship on my part, not to mention spawning a number of bandana-clad Hendrix clones on the local music scene.

The Fender™ Stratocaster, Hendrix's axe of choice, was *de rigueur* for those who had caught the Hendrix bug (see Figure 3). His was a powerful influence from a distant corner of the globe (Seattle, Washington to Cape Town, South Africa). Naïvely perhaps, I may have unconsciously felt a sense of solidarity with his (or Chas Chandler's, more precisely) bold choice of a racially and geographically disparate rhythm section (initially with Noel Redding and Mitch Mitchell, two white British musicians), integrated to my mind for the noble purpose of creating boundary-crossing music together.

Coming of age in Cape Town towards the end of the 1960s, as a budding musician I attended numerous live concerts within the burgeoning rock scene there. Generally speaking, these were 'whites-only' affairs in keeping with the segregationist policies of apartheid. Ten years earlier, the powers that were had begun to enforce these policies with the aim of preventing musical (and other) interactions across racial lines. By the time of the rock concerts my friends and I witnessed a decade later, segregation was more or less a *fait accompli*, with concert patrons seated in separate blocks (at venues like the Cape Town City Hall, Hartleyvale football stadium, the Luxurama theatre, and so on). In such

---

[102] When Lennon claimed that the band was more popular than Jesus, the local authorities reacted by banning all Beatles records from the airwaves.

**Figure 3** 1958 Fender Stratocaster. User: Lightburst, CC BY-SA 4.0 <https://creativecommons.org/licenses/by-sa/4.0>, via Wikimedia Commons.

circumstances, Hendrix' integrated band and their ground-breaking music spoke of the absurdity of the political circumstances under which South Africans were kept apart from one another.

As much as I was fascinated by rock music from the United States,[103] jazz musicians there also formed musically and socially integrated bands. Here I have in mind the example of Ornette Coleman, whose earliest recordings featured the white double bassist Charlie Haden, again an exemplar to my young mind of music's power to transcend what seemed to me arbitrary boundaries. I pestered my parents to buy me an electric guitar and, mostly self-taught, played this instrument in various garage bands until leaving school.

I soon realised that there were any number of better guitarists than I on the local scene: true showmen, brimming with the confidence and aplomb I lacked, technically more proficient and more than willing to strut their stuff in live performance. Without too much regret, I put the electric guitar aside and took up the bass guitar as my chosen vehicle for gigs. In retrospect, this was a wise

---

[103] Quicksilver Messenger Service, Moby Grape, Spirit, Grateful Dead, and so on.

decision, but the six-string guitar has remained very dear to my heart, and I try to maintain my technique on this instrument through daily practice.

The electric guitar presents a unique set of technical challenges and possibilities for sound production and modification. Its location within the broader stringed instrument family presents the guitarist with a wide range of haptic potentialities under the fingers, so to speak. By the nature of its layout, the guitar fingerboard allows for complex chords to sound simultaneously and for individual notes and chords to be modified while they sound.[104] Some possible interactions facilitated by its construction include techniques idiosyncratic to the guitar and stringed instruments in general, such as hammer-ons and pull-offs.[105] String bends and vibrato techniques, whereby the guitarist bends or applies rapid oscillating hand movement to the sounding string, are also available and more or less idiomatic to the instrument. In the case of a right-handed player, these techniques generally deploy the left hand for their execution.

Similarly, the right or 'picking' hand presents various opportunities for the musician. These include a choice of fingerstyle (using thumb and fingers), picks held between the index and middle finger, picks adapted for the thumb, and combinations of all these approaches. Each approach has spawned whole schools of expert players and is variously applicable within specific musical genres. 'Traditional' styles such as acoustic folk and country music adopt such techniques as finger-picking, flatpicking (see Andress 2020), and so on. In general, it seems fair to say that instrumental techniques shape and are shaped by developments within and across genres and vice versa. This claim suggests a conception of musical genres as dynamic and evolving and intimately connected with available technologies.

However, the true potential and versatility of this instrument reveal themselves when both hands work together, as is generally the case. Chords, arpeggios, rootless voicings combined with successively sounding roots, contrapuntal lines, and chords together: these are a few available musical approaches among many. Less commonly found are techniques such as tapping (in which the guitarist 'taps' the strings from above with both hands). This produces a more

---

[104] Under normal circumstances, such possibilities are not available to pianists or organists. Early in his career, while playing with Charles Lloyd, Keith Jarrett (1968) used a slide pressed against the piano strings as a kind of special effect.

[105] To execute a hammer-on, the guitarist produces a slur by fretting a successive higher note, generally on the same string. The converse applies to the pull-off, in which the higher note is succeeded by an adjacent note of lower pitch. These are examples of readily available legato phrasing, so that the guitarist phrase similarly to blown instruments, such as saxophone or trumpet. Not limited to single notes, the topography of the fretboard further enables such techniques to be applied to chords.

rhythmic, even percussive, and intricately complex sound and is exemplified in recordings by such master musicians as Stanley Jordan and Eddie van Halen.

*Scordatura*, in which the player adapts the instrument's conventional (E2 A2 D3 G3 B3 E3) tuning, yields further creative opportunities for the musician. There is a wide range of open tunings available, commonly used in folk music (Joni Mitchell, for example). Slide guitarists often deploy such tunings, so that the open guitar may be tuned to a major chord and the slide moved to produce successions of these chords, for example. Such approaches are sometimes found in early blues.

What might be termed wholesale *scordatura* occurs when the conventional open tuning (as just mentioned) is maintained but transposed to sound in a different key (down a whole step to D, for argument's sake).[106] The baritone guitar, for instance, adapts conventional guitar construction with a longer scale length and a heavier, enlarged body, sounding a fourth below open tuning (as B1 E2 A2 D3 F#3 B3).

A crucial aspect of the guitar and related instruments with fretboards is ease of transposition. The nature of the instrument lends itself to transposing a given fingering pattern (say, a major scale) to a new key, merely by moving the initial root note and using the identical fingering pattern to play it.[107] To accomplish the same task on a keyboard instrument necessitates changing fingerings accordingly.

This overview, detailing some affordances of the guitar, serves to underscore the way in which evolving instrument technologies have influenced musicking and vice versa. As such, it represents a slightly artificial attempt to capture some potential guitaristic affordances in isolation, ignoring real-world systems where other sound modifiers are brought into play, such as guitars combined with pedals and amplifiers.

The opportunity now arises to approach actual practice more closely, wherein such systems are routinely integrated into the moment of performance. In the case of well-known performers, such systems may be said to work together to produce a set of signature sounds which the audience may use to identify the stamp of a given individual or band.

My own practice is mildly unusual in that I play electric guitar finger-style. Possibly because of my history and preferences as a bassist, my choice has been to adopt a modified bass technique to the guitar (that is to say, not using a plectrum). Echoing Sudnow (2001: 125), 'My hands make it up as they go

---

[106] So-called drop D or D standard tuning, prevalent in genres such as death metal (https://studentofguitar.com/death-metal-tuning/, accessed 17 May 2023).

[107] See Sudnow (2001: 8–11) for major scale fingerings for piano.

along.' That said, guitarists use many combinations of plectrum and finger-style options in keeping with their individual preferences.

## Conclusion

While I have claimed that the embodied project presents a more accurate portrayal of individual and collective musicking than does classic CTM, it would be remiss of me not to mention objections to this project. Broadly speaking, the project's critics call for a more balanced account of the relationship between internal mental processes and external factors (Clark 2008; Rupert 2009; Shapiro 2019), based on rigorous scientific methods (Wilson and Golonka 2013).[108]

Towards the end of *Musicking*, Small (1998: 201–206) introduces a discussion of a solitary flute-player on the African savanna.[109] He presents this lone herdsman as a kind of outlier case, suggesting that this musician's activities take place in true isolation, and calling into question what relationships his playing might enact, since there are no other nearby humans to hear the melody he is playing.

Small's discussion traverses the technology of the home-made instrument, compared to its 'more advanced' Western counterpart the concert flute, and the nature, provenance, and style of the emergent melodies and their place in the musician's oral tradition. His conclusion is striking: 'Even to play a home-made flute, alone, with no one but oneself to hear, is an act that can define relationships that are just as complex as that of taking part with two thousand others in a symphony concert' (205–206).[110] If we accept his line of argument, it follows that even solitary musical activity unfolds against the background of a given tradition, however recent or ancient this may be.

Earlier I undertook to look for points of contact between enactivism and ecological psychology. While both enactivism and ecological psychology disclaim the necessity of representations as intermediaries in perception, there are significant differences between the two approaches such that: 'In Ecological Psychology direct perception and action is the basic way of knowing, and all other ways originate there. In Enactivism cognition is emergent out of sensori-motor coupling' (Read & Szokolszky 2020: 51).

---

[108] I am grateful to one of the anonymous peer reviewers for pointing this out.

[109] Small confesses that he was in two minds about including this discussion, with some colleagues advising against courting the risk of accusations of 'Othering' – the herdsman as 'a totalised representation' (201) – that this discussion might bring in its wake.

[110] So too Malafouris (2020: 4): 'The presence of the simplest artifact has the potential to alter the relationships between humans and their environments.'

These authors conclude that these different points of departure work against any convergence between these approaches; so too Heft (2020), maintaining that 'a synthesis of the two approaches is not possible' (23), and Felten (2020), who claims, 'One obstacle to such an ecological-enactive approach is the conceptual tension between the firm commitment to realism of those following James Gibson's ecological approach and the central tenet of enactivism that each living organism enacts its own world, interpreted as a constructivist or subjectivist position' (55).

Heras-Escribano (2019)[111] argues that ecological psychology's claim that the properties of affordances are directly perceived carries with it the implication that notions of computation (including representations and inferences) are unnecessary. Both ecological psychology (direct realism) and enactivism (constructivism) share common ground in their disdain for such notions, upon which concepts so much early computationalism depended.

The major stumbling block against a rapprochement between the two is ecological psychology's insistence on direct realism. While sympathetic to Gibson's exploration of the natural world (outside the laboratory), Bruce and Tadmor's (2015) critique (24ff.) of Gibson's 'high-level visual information processing when he proposed immediate and direct perception of the natural environment' starkly contrasts with the sense-making aspect of enactivism. Not all is lost, though, for in the same setting, Baggs et al. (2020) argue that

> One promising potential area of convergence between the ecological and enactive approaches in cognitive science is in the development of a general theory of skill learning. Theoretical work within both approaches has come increasingly, in recent years, to appeal to the notion of skill as an explanatory factor in the understanding of behavior. (138)

In describing aspects of my own practice (as gradual refinements to a set of musical skills), I have reflected on the ways in which my instruments of choice and their construction mechanics (their affordances, *tout court*) directly influence my engagements. While I have adopted a parsimonious attitude to such affordances, considering these as 'minimal' as a point of departure for the discussion, I have tried to situate these minimal affordances as embedded in my personal history and contributing to my sense of musical agency. Since even these minimal engagements involve a complex set of variables (for instance, embodiment, feedback, motor intentionality, the haptic and other sensory

---

[111] 'Affordances are the possibilities for action that are available to agents in their environments. According to their defenders, when we explore the environment we do not just perceive physical objects; rather, we also perceive what we can do with them: We perceive the graspability of a cup, the climbability of a step, or the kickability of a ball' (3).

systems, musical skills, among others), I have tried to avoid reducing these to their constituent elements but have attempted instead to respect their complex interactions by situating these within a transdisciplinary framework.

This framework incorporates music perception and cognition, Small's concept of musicking as action, participatory sense-making, enactive cognising, phenomenology, and systems theory, and metaphysical ideas of space and time. I am aware of the potential risk of seeming to cherry-pick ideas to suit the complexities of such musical practice but have tried to approach this complexity as irreducible to its components: in other words, to consider these aspects as starting from a full-bodied engagement with musicking. 'The feeling, sensing, and experiencing body is engaged with musical sounds and their consequences in many ways, whether we are aware of it or not. . . . [T]he body is not only an instrument through which musical thinking takes place; the body can be taken as a conscious and explicit *object of transformation*' (Westerlund & Juntunen 2010: 113, emphasis added).

Humans and artefacts have evolved together over time in a continuous process of mutual transformation, less a straightforward trajectory of progress than in fits and starts, more akin to the 'tinkering' that Spatz (2017) invokes. Experimental procedures of trial and error do not necessarily produce successful results at first attempt; these processes are rather considered as gradual incremental steps towards refinement. Hence, there emerges a process of mutual transformation wherein greater depth of knowledge transforms the affordances of a given tool, and vice versa. So too, with some conceptions of mind as transformational organic process[112] that have been sketched here.

Likewise, my own practice reveals how my musical learning processes have not been a simple matter of proceeding on a straight path from novice to professional. Clearly this may differ according to personal circumstances, but for me learning the idiosyncrasies of musical instruments has been beset by fits and starts, plenty of repetition on plateaux with occasional technical breakthroughs. This is a non-linear description of learning in keeping with the characterisations of complexity that systems theory describes.

In describing practice from the inside, I have tried to avoid the grand theories and courted self-indulgence that come by bringing in autobiographical elements (anecdotes, milestones on a personal journey, however one couches these). In principle, one's practice is personal, since its point of origin is a human being in a particular historical moment. The nature of this historical moment – within the brain-body-environment system against which processes of toolmaking (and

---

[112] For a contemporary account of the relevance of Bateson's process thinking to psychology, see Tempone-Wiltshire and Dowie (2023).

tool using) play out – seems to inspire Penny's (2017) insight that the 'painter's brush, the violinist's bow, the harvester's scythe, and so many other artifacts are complex and sophisticated devices because they have evolved in a deep structural coupling with the rhythms of bodies and sensorimotor loops, and are integrated into complex cultural practices' (268).

It seems profoundly mistaken to me to undervalue the complex relationships set in motion in and through musicking. 'Music has been widely (and very nearsightedly) accepted as a matter of cognitive understanding, or special intelligence, instead of a flesh-and-blood experience in which there is a continuum between various aspects of experience' (Westerlund & Juntunen 2010: 114–115). Regarding this continuum of experience, Di Paolo et al. (2021) eloquently sums up the central concerns of the enactive approach: ' Being alive, being a sensorimotor creature, being a potential incarnation of powers and sensitivities that have been historically developed in human communities, and being a participant in the historical transformation of the world. Taking all of these entangled dimensions into account is part of the desiderata of any truly embodied approach to human minds' (790). This seems a particularly fitting note on which to conclude this discussion.

# Bibliography

Agazarian, Y., & Gantt, S. (2005). The systems perspective. In *The Handbook of Group Research and Practice*. Thousand Oaks, CA: SAGE, 187–200.

Altenmüller, E., Furuya, S., Scholz, D. S., & Ioannou, C. I. (2018). Brain research in music performance. In Thaut, M. H., & Hodges, D. A., eds., *The Oxford Handbook of Music and the Brain*. Oxford Handbooks. Oxford: Oxford University Press, 459–486.

Anderson, M. L. (2003). Embodied cognition: A field guide. *Artificial Intelligence*, 149(1), 91–130.

Andress, T. (2020). Pick and fingerstyle technique. bit.ly/4fbu2L8, accessed 19 May 2023.

Arrow, H., McGrath, J. E., & Berdahl, J. L. (2000). *Small Groups as Complex Systems: Formation, Coordination, Development, and Adaptation*. Thousand Oaks, CA: SAGE.

Baggs, E., Raja, V., & Anderson, M. L. (2020). Extended skill learning. In Di Paolo, E. A., Chemero, A., Heras-Escribano, M., & McGann, M., eds., *Enaction and Ecological Psychology: Convergences and Complementarities*. Lausanne: Frontiers Media, 138–147.

Barclay, R. (2011). The development of musical instruments: National trends and musical implications. In Lawson, C., ed., *The Cambridge Companion to the Orchestra*. Cambridge: Cambridge University Press, 22–41.

Bardone, E. (2010). Affordances as abductive anchors. In Magnani, L., Carnielli, W., & Pizzi, C., eds., *Model-Based Reasoning in Science and Technology: Abduction, Logic and Computational Discovery*. Studies in Computational Intelligence, vol. 314. Berlin: Springer, 135–157.

Barrett, L. (2015). *Beyond the Brain: How Body and Environment Shape Animal and Human Minds*. Princeton, NJ: Princeton University Press.

Barrett, M. S., ed. (2014). *Collaborative Creative Thought and Practice in Music*. Farnham: Ashgate.

Bateson, G. (1972). *Steps to an Ecology of Mind: Collected Essays in Anthropology, Psychiatry, Evolution, and Epistemology*. Chicago, IL: University of Chicago Press.

Bateson, G. (1980). *Mind and Nature: A Necessary Unity*. New York, NY: Bantam Books.

Beer, R. D. (2008). The dynamics of brain–body–environment systems: A status report. In Calvo, P., & Gomila, A., eds., *Handbook of Cognitive Science: An Embodied Approach*. Amsterdam: Elsevier, 99–120.

Bertolaso, M., & Di Stefano, N., eds. (2017). *The Hand: Perception, Cognition, Action.* Studies in Applied Philosophy, Epistemology and Rational Ethics (SAPERE, volume 38). Cham: Springer.

Bogg, J., & Geyer, R., eds. (2017). *Complexity, Science and Society.* London: CRC Press.

Borgo, D. (2022). *Sync or Swarm: Improvising Music in a Complex Age.* Revised edition. New York, NY: Continuum.

Bowman, W. D. (1998). *Philosophical Perspectives on Music.* Oxford: Oxford University Press.

Bremmer, M., & Nijs, L. (2020). The role of the body in instrumental and vocal music pedagogy: A dynamical systems theory perspective on the music teacher's bodily engagement in teaching and learning. *Frontiers in Education,* 5(79). www.frontiersin.org/journals/education/articles/10.3389/feduc.2020.00079/full.

Brennan, M., Pignato, J. M., & Stadnicki, D. A., eds. (2021). *The Cambridge Companion to the Drum Kit.* Cambridge Companions to Music. Cambridge: Cambridge University Press.

Bresler, L., ed. (2007). *International Handbook of Research in Arts Education.* Part 1. Dordrecht: Springer.

Brown, R. M., Zatorre, R. J., & Penhune, V. B. (2015). Expert music performance: Cognitive, neural, and developmental bases. In Altenmüller, E., Finger, S., & Boller, F., eds., *Music, Neurology, and Neuroscience: Evolution, the Musical Brain, Medical Conditions, and Therapies.* Amsterdam: Elsevier B.V., 57–86.

Bruce, V. & Tadmor Y. (2015) Perception: Beyond Gibson (1950) direct perception. In Haslam, S. A., Slater, A. M., & Smith, J. R, eds., *Cognitive Psychology: Revisiting the Classic Studies.* London: SAGE, 24–37.

Bruford, B. (2018). *Uncharted: Creativity and the Expert Drummer.* Ann Arbor, MI: University of Michigan Press.

Calvo, P., & Gomila, A., eds. (2008). *Handbook of Cognitive Science: An Embodied Approach.* Amsterdam: Elsevier.

Capra, F., & Luisi, P. L. (2014). *The Systems View of Life: A Unifying Vision.* Cambridge: Cambridge University Press.

Carvalho, J. M. (2019). Music and emergence. In Grimshaw-Aagaard, M., Walther-Hansen, M., & Knakkergaard, M., eds., *The Oxford Handbook of Sound and Imagination, vol II.* Oxford: Oxford University Press, 77–95.

Cassam, Q. (2011). The embodied self. In Gallagher, S., ed. *The Oxford Handbook of the Self.* Oxford: Oxford University Press, 139–158.

Chemero, A. (2003). An outline of a theory of affordances. *Ecological Psychology,* 15(2), 181–195. DOI: https://doi.org/10.1207/S15326969ECO1502_5.

Chillón, J. M. (2017). Ready-to-hand in Heidegger. Philosophy as an everyday understanding of the world and the question concerning technology. In Bertolaso, M., & Di Stefano, N., eds., *The Hand: Perception, Cognition, Action*. Studies in Applied Philosophy, Epistemology and Rational Ethics. Cham: Springer, 115–126.

Clark, A. (1998). *Being There: Putting Brain, Body, and World Together Again*. Cambridge, MA: MIT Press.

Clark, A. (2008). *Supersizing the Mind: Embodiment, Action, and Cognitive Extension*. Oxford: Oxford University Press.

Clarke, E. F. (2005). *Ways of Listening*. Oxford: Oxford University Press.

Clifton, T. (1983). *Music as Heard: A Study in Applied Phenomenology*. New Haven, CT: Yale University Press.

Cobussen, M. (2017). *The Field of Musical Improvisation*. Leiden: University of Leiden Press.

Cohen, R. S., & Wartofsky, M. W. (1980). Editorial preface. In Maturana, H. R., & Varela, F. J. *Autopoiesis and Cognition: The Realization of the Living*. Dordrecht: D. Reidel.

Crecraft, D. I., & Gergely, S. (2002). Signals and signal processing. In *Analog Electronics Circuits, Systems and Signal Processing*. Oxford: Butterworth-Heinemann, 13–71.

Cross, I. (2007). Music and cognitive evolution. In Dunbar, R. I. M., & Barrett, L., eds., *The Oxford Handbook of Evolutionary Psychology*. Oxford: Oxford University Press, 649–667.

Cross, I., & Morley, I. (2010). The evolution of music: Theories, definitions and the nature of the evidence. In Malloch, S., & Trevarthen, C., eds., *Communicative Musicality: Exploring the Basis of Human Companionship*. Oxford: Oxford University Press, 61–81.

Dailey, D. J. (2011). *Electronics for Guitarists*. New York, NY: Springer.

Damasio, A. (1994). *Descartes' Error: Emotion, Reason and the Human Brain*. London: Vintage Books.

Damasio, A. (2004). *Looking for Spinoza: Joy, Sorrow and the Feeling Brain*. London: Vintage.

Damasio, A. (2010). *Self Comes to Mind: Constructing the Conscious Brain*. London: William Heinemann.

DeNora, T. (2014). *Making Sense of Reality: Culture and Perception in Everyday Life*. London: SAGE.

De Souza, J. (2017). *Music at Hand: Instruments, Bodies, and Cognition*. Oxford: Oxford University Press.

Di Paolo, E. A., Rohde, M., & De Jaegher, H. (2014). Horizons for the enactive mind: Values, social interaction, and play. In Stewart, J., Gapenne, O., & Di

Paolo, A. E., eds., *Enaction: Toward a New Paradigm for Cognitive Science.* Cambridge, MA: MIT Press, 33–87.

Di Paolo, E. A., Heras-Escribano, M., Chemero, A., & McGann, M., eds. (2021). *Enaction and Ecological Psychology: Convergences and Complementarities.* Lausanne: Frontiers Media.

Dieleman, H. (2012). Transdisciplinary artful doing in spaces of experimentation and imagination. *Transdisciplinary Journal of Engineering & Science*, 3, 44–57.

Dokic, J. (2010). Perceptual recognition and the feeling of presence. In Nanay, B., ed., *Perceiving the World* (online ed., Oxford Academic, 1 January 2011). DOI: https://doi.org/10.1093/acprof:oso/9780195386196.003.0003, accessed 7 June 2023.

Dove, G. (2022). *Abstract Concepts and the Embodied Mind: Rethinking Grounded Cognition.* Oxford: Oxford University Press.

Dowling, W. J. (1993). Procedural and declarative knowledge in music cognition and education. In Tighe, T. J., & Dowling, W. J., eds., *Psychology and Music: The Understanding of Melody and Rhythm.* Mahwah, NJ: Lawrence Erlbaum, 5–18.

Dreyfus, H. L. (2002). Intelligence without representation – Merleau-Ponty's critique of mental representation: The relevance of phenomenology to scientific explanation. *Phenomenology and the Cognitive Sciences* 1, 367–383.

Duby, M. (2016). 'Fanfare for the warriors': Jazz, education, and state control in 1980s South Africa and after. In Johnson, B., ed., *Jazz and Totalitarianism.* New York: Routledge, 288–314.

Duby, M. (2019). Affordances in real, virtual, and imaginary musical performance. In Grimshaw-Aagaard, M., Walther-Hansen, M., & Knakkergaard, M., eds., *The Oxford Handbook of Sound and Imagination, vol II.* Oxford: Oxford University Press, 96–114.

Duby, M. (2020). Minds, music, and motion: Ecologies of ensemble performance. *Music and Practice*, 6. DOI: https://doi.org/10.32063/0607.

Duby, M. (2022a). The ethics of teamwork: Notes on a South African recording project. In Kahr, M., ed., *Artistic Practice as Research in Jazz: Positions, Theories, Methods.* New York, NY: Routledge.

Duby, M. (2022b). Enactive cognition in improvising musical ensembles: A South African perspective. In Lauwrens, J., ed., *Embodiment and the Arts: Views from South Africa.* Pretoria: Pretoria University Law Press.

Dunbar, R. I. M., & Barrett, L., eds. (2017). *The Oxford Handbook of Evolutionary Psychology.* Oxford: Oxford University Press.

Elliott, D. J., ed. (2010). *Praxial Music Education: Reflections and Dialogues.* Oxford Scholarship Online, accessed 7 June 2023. DOI: https://doi.org/ 10.1093/acprof:oso/9780195385076.001.0001.

Ericsson, K. A., Hoffman, R. R., Kozbelt, A., & Williams, A. M., eds. (2018). *The Cambridge Handbook of Expertise and Expert Performance.* 2nd edition. Cambridge: Cambridge University Press.

Eysenck, M. W., & Groome, D., eds. (2015). *Cognitive Psychology: Revisiting the Classic Studies.* London: SAGE.

Felten, T. E. (2020). Mind after Uexküll: A foray into the worlds of ecological psychologists and enactivists. In Di Paolo, E. A., Heras-Escribano, M., Chemero, A., & McGann, M., eds. (2021). *Enaction and Ecological Psychology: Convergences and Complementarities.* Lausanne: Frontiers Media.

Ferroni, F., and Gallese, V. (2023). Social bodily self: Conceptual and psychopathological considerations. In Alsmith, A. J. T., & Longo, M. R., eds., *The Routledge Handbook of Bodily Awareness.* Abingdon: Routledge. 522–541.

Frankish, K., & Ramsey, W. L., eds. (2012). *The Cambridge Handbook of Cognitive Science.* Cambridge: Cambridge University Press.

Froese, T. (2010). From cybernetics to second-order cybernetics: A comparative analysis of their central ideas. *Constructivist Foundations*, 5(2), 75–85.

Froese, T. (2012). Sense-making with a little help from my friends: Introducing Ezequiel Di Paolo and Hanne De Jaegher. *Avant* III(2), 143–146.

Fuchs, T. (2011). The brain: A mediating organ. *Journal of Consciousness Studies*, 18(7–8), 196–221.

Fuchs, T. (2021). *In Defense of the Human Being: Foundational Questions of an Embodied Anthropology.* Oxford: Oxford University Press.

Fuster, J. M. (2010). Functional neuroanatomy of executive process. In Gurd, J., Kischka, U., & Marshall, J., eds. *The Handbook of Clinical Neuropsychology.* 2nd ed. Oxford: Oxford University Press, 822–834.

Fuster, J. M. (2013). *The Neuroscience of Freedom and Creativity: Our Predictive Brain.* Cambridge: Cambridge University Press.

Gabora, L., & Ranjan, A. (2013). How insight emerges in a distributed, content-addressable memory. In Vartanian, O., Bristol, A. S., & Kaufman, J. C., eds., *Neuroscience of Creativity.* Cambridge, MA: MIT Press, 19–43.

Gallagher, S. (1997). Mutual enlightenment: Recent phenomenology in cognitive science. *Journal of Consciousness Studies*, 4(3), 195–214.

Gallagher, S. (2009). Philosophical antecedents of situated cognition. In Robbins, P., & Aydede, M., eds., *The Cambridge Handbook of Situated*

*Cognition*. Cambridge Handbooks in Psychology. Cambridge: Cambridge University Press. Kindle Edition. 35–51.

Gallagher, S., ed. (2011). *The Oxford Handbook of the Self*. Oxford: Oxford University Press.

Gallagher, S. (2020). *Action and Interaction*. Oxford: Oxford University Press.

Geeves, A., & Sutton, J. (2014). Embodied cognition, perception, and performance in music. *Empirical Musicology Review*, 9(3–4), 247–253.

Gibson, J. J. (1962). Observations on active touch. *Psychological Review*, 69(6), 477–91.

Gibson, J. J. (1966). *The Senses Considered as Perceptual Systems*. London: George Allen & Unwin Ltd.

Gibson, J. J. (2015). *The Ecological Approach to Visual Perception*, Classic Edition. New York: Psychology Press.

Goldfield, E. C. (1995) *Emergent Forms: Origins and Early Development of Human Action and Perception*. New York: Oxford University Press.

Goldsmith, M. (2015). *Sound: A Very Short Introduction*. Oxford: Oxford University Press.

Grimshaw-Aagaard, M., Walther-Hansen, M., & Knakkergaard, M., eds. (2019). *The Oxford Handbook of Sound and Imagination, vol II*. Oxford: Oxford University Press.

Hallowell, R. (2009). Humberto Maturana and Francisco Varela's contribution to media ecology: Autopoiesis, the Santiago school of cognition, and enactive cognitive science. *Proceedings of the Media Ecology Association*, 10, 143–158.

Hatfield, G. (2018). 'René Descartes', *The Stanford Encyclopedia of Philosophy* (Summer Edition), Edward N. Zalta (ed.), https://plato.stanford.edu/archives/sum2018/entries/descartes/, accessed 6 September 2022.

Hayles, K. N., ed. (1991). *Chaos and Order: Complex Dynamics in Literature and Science*. Chicago, IL: University of Chicago Press.

Hayles, K. N. (1999). *How We Became Posthuman: Virtual Bodies in Cybernetics, Literature, and Informatics*. Chicago, IL: University of Chicago Press.

Hayles, K. N. (2017). *Unthought: The Power of the Cognitive Nonconscious*. Chicago, IL: University of Chicago Press.

Heft, H. (2001). *Ecological Psychology in Context: James Gibson, Roger Barker, and the Legacy of William James's Radical Empiricism*. Hove: Psychology Press.

Heft, H. (2007). The social constitution of perceiver-environment reciprocity. *Ecological Psychology*, 19(2), 37–41.

Heras-Escribano, M. (2019). *The Philosophy of Affordances*. New Directions in Philosophy and Cognitive Science. Cham: Palgrave Macmillan.

Heylighen, F., & Joslyn, C. (2001). Cybernetics and second-order cybernetics. In Meyers, R. A., ed., *Encyclopedia of Physical Science & Technology*. 3rd ed. New York: Academic Press, 155–169.

Heylighen, F., Cilliers, P., & Gershenson, C. (2017). Philosophy and complexity. In Bogg, J., & Geyer, R., eds., *Complexity, Science and Society*. London: CRC Press.

Hintikka, J. (2006). The phenomenological dimension. In Smith, B., & Smith, W. D., eds., *The Cambridge Companion to Husserl*. Cambridge: Cambridge University Press, 78–105.

Holyoak, K. J., & Morrison, R. J., eds. (2012). *The Oxford Handbook of Thinking and Reasoning*. Oxford Library of Psychology. Oxford: Oxford University Press.

Hoppe, C., & Müller, S. A., eds. (2021). *Music in the Body – Body in Music*. Göttingen Studies in Musicology. Hildesheim: Georg Olms Verlag.

Hutchins, E. (1995). *Cognition in the Wild*. Cambridge, MA: MIT Press.

Hutchins, E. (2005). Material anchors for conceptual blends. *Journal of Pragmatics*, 37(10), 1555–1577.

Iyer, V. (2002). Embodied mind, situated cognition, and expressive microtiming in African-American Music. *Music Perception* 19(3), 387–414.

Jantsch, E. (1980). *The Self-Organizing Universe: Scientific and Human Implications of the Emerging Paradigm of Evolution*. Systems Science and World Order Library. Oxford: Pergamon Press.

Jensenius, A. R. (2022). *Sound Actions: Conceptualizing Musical Instruments*. Cambridge, MA: MIT Press.

Johnson, M. L. (2007). *The Meaning of the Body: Aesthetics of Human Understanding*. Chicago, IL: University of Chicago Press.

Johnson, M. L., & Larson, S. (2003). 'Something in the way she moves': Metaphors of musical motion. *Metaphor & Symbol* 18(2), 63–84.

Kahn, D. (2017). Sound leads elsewhere. In Cobussen, M., Meelberg, V., & Truax, B., eds., *The Routledge Companion to Sounding Art*. New York, NY: Routledge, 41–50.

Kelso, J. A. S. (2003). Cognitive coordination dynamics. In Tschacher, W., & Dauwalder, J.-P., eds., *The Dynamical Systems Approach to Cognition: Concepts and Empirical Paradigms Based on Self-Organization, Embodiment, and Coordination Dynamics*. Studies of Nonlinear Phenomena in Life Science. Singapore: World Scientific Publishing, 45–67. DOI: https://doi.org/10.1080/05679320500212114.

Kim, Y., & Gilman, S. L., eds. (2018). *The Oxford Handbook of Music and the Body*. Oxford Handbooks. Oxford: Oxford University Press.

Kiverstein, J., & Rietveld, E. (2020). Scaling-up skilled intentionality to linguistic thought. *Synthese*, 198 (Suppl 1), 175–194. DOI: https://doi.org/10.1007/s11229-020-02540-3.

Lagomarsino, V. (2019). Exploring the underground network of trees: The nervous system of the forest. https://sitn.hms.harvard.edu/flash/2019/exploring-the-underground-network-of-trees-the-nervous-system-of-the-forest/#:~:text=Dendrologists%2C%20scientists%20who%20study%20wooded,a%20technique%20called%20isotope%20tracing, accessed 10 June 2023.

Langer, S. K. (1948). *Philosophy in a New Key: A Study in the Symbolism of Reason, Rite and Art*. New York, NY: Mentor Books.

Larkin, C. (2006). *The Encyclopedia of Popular Music*. 4th ed. Oxford: Oxford University Press. DOI: https://doi.org/10.1093/acref/9780195313734.001.0001.

Lauwrens, J., ed. (2022). *Embodiment and the Arts: Views from South Africa*. Pretoria: Pretoria University Law Press.

Lave, J. (1991). Situating learning in communities of practice. In Resnick, L. B., Levine, J. M., & S. D. Teasley, eds., *Perspectives on Socially Shared Cognition*. American Psychological Association, 63–82. DOI: https://doi.org/10.1037/10096-003.

Lave, J. (2008). Epilogue: Situated learning and changing practice. In Amin, A., & Roberts, J., eds., *Community, Economic Creativity, and Organization*. Oxford Scholarship Online, 283–296.

Lawson, C., ed. (2018). *The Cambridge Companion to the Orchestra*. Cambridge: Cambridge University Press.

Legrand, D. (2011). Phenomenological dimensions of bodily self-consciousness. In Gallagher, S., ed., *The Oxford Handbook of the Self*. Oxford: Oxford University Press, 204–229.

Lehmann, A. C., Gruber, H., & Kopiez, R. (2018). Expertise in music. In Ericsson, K. A., Hoffman, R. R., Kozbelt, A., & Williams, A. M., eds., *The Cambridge Handbook of Expertise and Expert Performance*. 2nd ed. Cambridge: Cambridge University Press, 535–549.

Leman, M. (2008). *Embodied Music Cognition and Mediation Technology*. Cambridge, MA: MIT Press.

Leman, M., Nijs, L., & Di Stefano, N. (2017). On the role of the hand in the expression of music. In Bertolaso, M., & Di Stefano, N., eds., *The Hand: Perception, Cognition, Action*. Studies in Applied Philosophy, Epistemology and Rational Ethics. Cham: Springer, 175–192.

Lerner, R. M., ed. (2006). *Handbook of Child Psychology: Vol 1, Theoretical Models of Human Development*. 6th ed. Hoboken, NJ: John Wiley and Sons, Inc.

Lesaffre, M., Maes, P-J., & Leman, M., eds. (2017). *The Routledge Companion to Embodied Music Interaction*. New York, NY: Routledge.

Lettvin, J. Y., Maturana, H. R., McCulloch, W. S., & Pitts, W. H. (1959). What the frog's eye tells the frog's brain. *Proceedings of the IRE*, 1940–1951.

Lineweaver, C., Davies, P., & Ruse, M., eds. (2013). *Complexity and the Arrow of Time*. Cambridge: Cambridge University Press.

Luhmann, N. (2013). *Introduction to Systems Theory*. Translated by Dirk Baecker. Cambridge: Polity Press.

Malafouris, L. (2013). *How Things Shape the Mind: A Theory of Material Engagement*. Cambridge, MA: MIT Press.

Malafouris, L. (2020). Thinking as 'Thinging': Psychology with Things. *Current Directions in Psychological Science*, 29, 1, 3–8.

Malloch, S., & Trevarthen, C., eds. (2009). *Communicative Musicality: Exploring the Basis of Human Companionship*. Oxford: Oxford University Press.

Malone, T. W., & Bernstein, M. S. (2015) *Handbook of Collective Intelligence*. Cambridge, MA: MIT Press.

Marin, M. M., & Peltzer-Karpf, A. (2009). Towards a dynamic systems approach to the development of language and music: Theoretical foundations and methodological issues. In Louhivuori, J., Eerola, T., Saarikallio, S., Himberg, T., & Eerola, P-S., eds., *Proceedings of the 7th Triennial Conference of European Society for the Cognitive Sciences of Music* (ESCOM 2009). Jyväskylä, Finland, 284–292. https://jyx.jyu.fi/handle/123456789/20138.

Maturana, H. R., & Varela, F. J. (1980). *Autopoiesis and Cognition: The Realization of the Living*. Dordrecht: D. Reidel Publishing Company.

Maturana, H. R., & Varela, F. J. (1998). *The Tree of Knowledge: The Biological Roots of Human Understanding*. Revised edition. Boulder, CO: Shambhala.

McAuliffe, S., & Malpas, J. (2022). Improvising the Round Dance of Being: Reading Heidegger from a Musical Perspective. In Rentmeester, C., & Warren, J. R., eds., *Heidegger and Music*. New Heidegger Research. Lanham: Rowman & Littlefield Publishers.

McGinn, C. (2015). *Prehension: The Hand and the Emergence of Humanity*. Cambridge, MA: MIT Press.

McIntyre, P. (2013). Creativity as a system in action. In Thomas, K., & Chan, J., eds., *Handbook of Research on Creativity*. 84–97. Cheltenham, UK: Edward Elgar Publishing.

Meadows, D. (2008). *Thinking in Systems: A Primer*. Edited by L. Wright. White River Junction, VT: Chelsea Green Publishing.

Menary, R. (2007). *Cognitive Integration: Mind and Cognition Unbounded*. New Directions in Philosophy and Cognitive Science. Basingstoke: Palgrave Macmillan.

Merleau-Ponty, M. (2002). *Phenomenology of Perception*. Translated by Colin Smith. Routledge Classics. London: Routledge.

Michaels, C. F., Weier, Z., & Harrison, S. J. (2007). Using vision and dynamic touch to perceive the affordances of tools. *Perception*, 36(5), 750–772.

Miller, C. (1998). Interview with Merton Barrow. University of Cape Town, Islandora Collection. https://digitalcollections.lib.uct.ac.za/interview-merton-barrow, accessed 21 June 2023.

Montague, E. (2018). Entrainment and embodiment in musical performance. In Kim, Y., & Gilman, S. L., eds., *The Oxford Handbook of Music and the Body*. Oxford Handbooks. Oxford: Oxford University Press, 177–192.

Montuori, A. (2022). Integrative transdisciplinarity: Explorations and experiments in creative scholarship. *Transdisciplinary Journal of Engineering & Science*, 13, 161–183.

Newen, A., De Bruin, L., & Gallagher, S., eds. (2018). *The Oxford Handbook of 4E Cognition*. Oxford Library of Psychology. Oxford: Oxford University Press.

Nicolescu, B. (2010). Methodology of transdisciplinarity: Levels of reality, logic of the included middle and complexity. *Transdisciplinary Journal of Engineering & Science*, 1, 17–32.

Noë, A. (2015). *Strange Tools: Art and Human Nature*. New York, NY: Hill and Wang.

O'Callaghan, C. (2007). *Sounds: A Philosophical Theory*. Oxford: Oxford University Press.

O'Callaghan, C. (2012). Perception. In Frankish, K., & Ramsey, W. L., eds., *The Cambridge Handbook of Cognitive Science*. Cambridge: Cambridge University Press, 73–91.

O'Callaghan, C. (2017). Grades of multisensory awareness. *Mind & Language*, 32, 155–181.

Pacherie, E. (2018). Motor intentionality. In Newen, A., De Bruin, L., & Gallagher, S., eds., *The Oxford Handbook of 4E Cognition*. Oxford Library of Psychology. Oxford: Oxford University Press, 369–388.

Penny, S. (2017). *Making Sense: Cognition, Computing, Art, and Embodiment.* Cambridge, MA: MIT Press.

Prigogine, I., & Stengers, I. (2017). *Order Out of Chaos: Man's New Dialogue with Nature.* Radical Thinkers. London: Verso.

Radman, Z., ed. (2013). *The Hand, an Organ of the Mind: What the Manual Tells the Mental.* Cambridge, MA: MIT Press.

Raimondi, V. (2019). The bio-logic of languaging and its epistemological background. *Language Sciences*, 71, 19–26.

Read, K., & Szokolszky, A. (2020). Ecological psychology and enactivism: Perceptually-guided action vs. sensation-based enaction. In Di Paolo, E. A., Heras-Escribano, M., Chemero, A., & McGann, M., eds. (2021). *Enaction and Ecological Psychology: Convergences and Complementarities.* Lausanne: Frontiers Media.

Rentmeester, C., & Warren, J. R., eds. (2023). *Heidegger and Music.* New Heidegger Research. Lanham: Rowman & Littlefield Publishers.

Rescorla, M. (2020). The computational theory of mind. In Edward N. Zalta (ed.), The Stanford Encyclopedia of Philosophy (Fall Edition). https://plato.stanford.edu/archives/fall2020/entries/computational-mind/, accessed 27 March 2024.

Reybrouck, M. (2021). *Musical Sense-Making: Enaction, Experience, and Computation.* New York: Routledge.

Richardson, K. (2010). *The Evolution of Intelligent Systems: How Molecules Became Minds.* Basingstoke: Palgrave Macmillan. DOI: https://doi.org/10.1057/9780230299245.

Richardson, M. J., & Chemero, A. (2014). Complex dynamical systems and embodiment. In L. Shapiro, ed., *The Routledge Handbook of Embodied Cognition.* London: Routledge, 39–50.

Rietveld, E. (2008). Situated normativity: The normative aspect of embodied cognition in unreflective action. *Mind*, 117, 973–1001.

Robbins, P., and Aydede, M. (2009). A short primer on embodied cognition. In Robbins, P., & Aydede, M., eds., *The Cambridge Handbook of Situated Cognition.* Cambridge Handbooks in Psychology. Cambridge: Cambridge University Press, 3–10.

Rupert, R. D. (2009). *Cognitive Systems and the Extended Mind.* Oxford: Oxford University Press.

Schiavio, A., & De Jaegher, H. (2017). Participatory sense-making in joint musical practice. In Lesaffre, M., Maes, P-J., & Leman, M., eds., *The Routledge Companion to Embodied Music Interaction.* New York, NY: Routledge, 31–39.

Schiavio, A., Ryan, K., Moran, N., van der Schyff, D., & Gallagher, S. (2023). By myself but not alone: Agency, creativity and extended musical historicity. *Journal of the Royal Musical Association*, 147/2, 533–556.

Segundo-Ortin, M., & Heras-Escribano, M. (2023). The risk of trivializing affordances: Mental and cognitive affordances examined. *Philosophical Psychology* 37(7), 1639–1655.

Selinger, E. M., & Crease,, R. P. (2002). Dreyfus on expertise: The limits of phenomenological analysis. *Continental Philosophy Review*, 34(3), 245–279.

Semin, G. R., Garrido, M. V., & Palma, T. A. (2012). Socially situated cognition: Recasting social cognition as an emergent phenomenon. In Fiske, S. T., & Macrae, C. N., eds., *The SAGE Handbook of Social Cognition*. London: SAGE, 138–165.

Shapiro, L. (2019). *Embodied Cognition*. 2nd ed. London: Routledge.

Sheets-Johnstone, M. (2011). *The Primacy of Movement*. Expanded 2nd ed. Amsterdam: John Benjamins Publishing Company.

Small, C. (1998). *Musicking: The Meanings of Performing and Listening*. Middletown, CT: Wesleyan University Press.

Smith, G. D. (2021). A window into my soul: Eudaimonia and autotelic drumming. In Brennan, M., Pignato, J. M., & Stadnicki, D. A., eds., *The Cambridge Companion to the Drum Kit*. Cambridge Companions to Music. Cambridge: Cambridge University Press, 248–258. DOI: https://doi.org/10.1017/9781108779517.023.

Smith, G. D. (2022). *A Philosophy of Playing Drum Kit: Magical Nexus*. Elements in Twenty-First Century Music Practice. Cambridge: Cambridge University Press. DOI: https://doi.org/10.1017/9781108993180.

Smith, H., & Dean, R. T., eds. (2009). *Practice-Led Research, Research-Led Practice in the Creative Arts*. Edinburgh: Edinburgh University Press.

Solé, R., & Levin, S. (2022). Ecological complexity and the biosphere: The next 30 years. *Philosophical Transactions of the Royal Society B*, 377, 20210376. DOI: https://doi.org/10.1098/rstb.2021.0376.

Spatz, B. (2017). Embodiment as first affordance: Tinkering, tuning, tracking. *Performance Philosophy*, 2(2), 256–271.

Stewart, J. (2014). Foundational issues in enaction as a paradigm for cognitive science: From the origin of life to consciousness and writing. In Stewart, J., Gapenne, O., & Di Paolo, A. E., eds., *Enaction: Toward a New Paradigm for Cognitive Science*. Cambridge, MA: MIT Press, 1–31.

Stewart, J., Gapenne, O., & Di Paolo, A. E., eds. (2014). *Enaction: Toward a New Paradigm for Cognitive Science*. Cambridge, MA: MIT Press.

Sudnow, D. (2001). *Ways of the Hand: A Rewritten Account*. Cambridge, MA: MIT Press.

Swanwick, K. (2007). Interlude 31: Metaphor and the mission of the arts. In Bresler, L., ed., *International Handbook of Research in Arts Education, Part 1*. Dordrecht: Springer.

Tan, D. (2015). Review of Eric Clarke, ways of listening: An ecological approach to the perception of musical meaning (Oxford University Press, 2005; paperback, 2011). *Music Theory Online*, 21, 3. DOI: https://doi.org/10.30535/mto.21.3.14.

Tanaka, A., & Donnarumma, M. (2018). The body as musical instrument. In Kim, Y., & Gilman, S. L., eds. *The Oxford Handbook of Music and the Body*. Oxford: Oxford University Press, 79–96.

Tempone-Wiltshire, J., & Dowie, T. (2023). Bateson's process ontology for psychological practice. *Process Studies*, 52(1), 95–116.

Thelen, E., & Smith, L. B. (2006). Dynamic Systems Theories. In Lerner, R. M., ed., *Handbook of Child Psychology: Vol 1, Theoretical Models of Human Development*. 6th ed. Hoboken, NJ: John Wiley and Sons, Inc., 258–312. DOI: https://doi.org/10.1002/9780470147658.chpsy0106.

Thompson, E. (2007). *Mind in Life: Biology, Phenomenology and the Sciences of Mind*. Cambridge, MA: Harvard University Press.

Thompson, W. F., & Ammirante, P. (2012). Musical thought. In Holyoak, K. J., & Morrison, R. J., eds., *The Oxford Handbook of Thinking and Reasoning*. Oxford Library of Psychology. Oxford: Oxford University Press, 774–788.

Van der Schyff, D., Schiavio, A., & Elliott, D. J. (2022). *Musical Bodies, Musical Minds: Enactive Cognitive Science and the Meaning of Human Musicality*. Cambridge, MA: MIT Press.

Van Manen, M. (2023). *Phenomenology of Practice: Meaning-Giving Methods in Phenomenological Research and Writing*. 2nd ed. New York, NY: Routledge.

Varela, F. J., Thompson, E., & Rosch, E. (2016). *The Embodied Mind: Cognitive Science and Human Experience*. Revised edition. Cambridge, MA: MIT Press.

Vartanian, O., Bristol, A. S., & Kaufman, J. C., eds. (2013). *Neuroscience of Creativity*. Cambridge, MA: MIT Press.

Vlassis, N. (2022). *A Concise Introduction to Multiagent Systems and Distributed Artificial Intelligence*. Synthesis Lectures on Artificial Intelligence and Machine Learning. Switzerland: Springer Nature.

Von Bertalanffy, L. (1968). *General Systems Theory: Foundations, Development, Applications*. Revised edition. New York, NY: George Braziller.

Von Foerster, H. (2003). *Understanding Understanding: Essays on Cybernetics and Cognition*. New York, NY: Springer.

von Uexküll, J. (2010). *A Foray into the Worlds of Animals and Humans, with a Theory of Meaning.* Translated by J. D. O'Neil. Minneapolis, MN: University of Minnesota Press.

Wenger, E. (1998). *Communities of Practice: Learning, Meaning, and Identity.* Learning in Doing: Social, Cognitive and Computational Perspectives. Cambridge: Cambridge University Press. DOI: https://doi.org/10.1017/CBO9780511803932.

Westerlund, H., & Juntunen, M. (2010). Music and knowledge in bodily experience. In Elliott, D. J., ed., *Praxial Music Education: Reflections and Dialogues.* Oxford Scholarship Online. 112–122. https://0-doi-org.oasis.unisa.ac.za/10.1093/acprof:oso/9780195385076.001.0001, accessed 7 June 2023.

Westney, W. (2006). *The Perfect Wrong Note: Learning to Trust Your Musical Self.* Pompton Plains, NJ: Amadeus Press.

Whyton, T. (2010). *Jazz Icons: Heroes, Myths and the Jazz Tradition.* Cambridge: Cambridge University Press.

Wilson, A. D., & Golonka, S. (2013). Embodied cognition is not what you think it is. *Frontiers in Psychology,* 4, 58.

Wilson, F. R. (1999). *The Hand: How Its Use Shapes the Brain, Language, and Human Culture.* New York, NY: Vintage Books.

Windsor, W. L. (2011). Gestures in music-making: Action, information and perception. In King, E. & Gritten, A., eds. *New Perspectives on Music and Gesture.* London: Routledge, 45–66.

Windsor W. L., & de Bézenac, C. (2012). Music and affordances. *Musicae Scientiae* 16(1), 102–120.

Wittmann, M. (2016). *Felt Time: The Psychology of How We Perceive Time.* Cambridge, MA: MIT Press.

Zahidi, K. (2013). Perception and the senses: A non-representational account. Unpublished doctoral thesis, University of Antwerp.

Zhang, J., & Patel, V. L. (2006). Distributed cognition, representation, and affordance. *Pragmatics & Cognition* 14(2), 333–341. DOI: https://doi.org/10.1075/pc.14.2.12zha.

# Select Discography and Videography

Andress, T. (1990). *Reckless Precision*. CD. Windham Hill Jazz 377054–2.

Bates, D. (1998). *Quiet Nights*. CD. Screwgun Records screwu 70007.

The Beatles. (1967). *Sergeant Pepper's Lonely Hearts Club Band*. Parlophone PCSJ 7027.

Cream. (1968). *Wheels of Fire*. ATCO Records SD 2–700.

Crispell, M. (2002). *A Pianist's Guide to Free Improvisation: Keys to Unlocking your Creativity*. DVD. Homespun CRI-KB21.

Jarrett, K. (1968). *Directions: In the Charles Lloyd Mood*. DVD. Stars of Jazz 2869042.

Pastorius, J. (1976). *Jaco Pastorius*. Epic EPC 81453.

Pastorius, J. (1998). *Honestly*. CD. Jazzpoint Records JP 1032.

Phillips, B. (1970/2021). *Basse Barre*. Cherry Red Records.

The Jimi Hendrix Experience. (1967). *Are You Experienced*. Reprise RS 6261.

Weber, E. (1975). *Yellow Fields*. ECM 1066.

Weber, E. (1993). *Pendulum*. ECM 1518.

Weber, E. (2012). *Résumé*. ECM 2051.

# Acknowledgements

I thank Simon Zagorski-Thomas for soliciting this manuscript in his role as series editor for Elements in Twenty-First Century Music Practice. Further, my grateful thanks go to the anonymous peer reviewers and my colleagues Simon Penny and Jorge Soto-Andrade for their comments, as well as to Dor Abrahamson and colleagues in the Embodied Design Research Laboratory at University of California (Berkeley). Attending their online postgraduate seminars and the ensuing discussions by various distinguished presenters enabled me to rehearse some of the ideas presented here in a supportive forum.

First and foremost my thanks go to my postgraduate students, among whom Maurice Azzano, Graeme Currie, Hugo de Waal, David Roman, Werner Spies, Milton van Wyk, and Ambigay Yudkoff. I further acknowledge the following researchers and musicians for their inspiring work: Melissa Bremmer, Bill Bruford, Marcel Cobussen, Rolf Inge Godøy, Vijay Iyer, Michael Kimmel, Lambros Malafouris, Luc Nijs, Maxine Sheets-Johnstone, and John Sutton.

The Academic and Non-Fiction Authors Association of South Africa (ANFASA) provided much appreciated financial support through a writing grant. The support of the National Research Foundation of South Africa (NRF) is also acknowledged.

*For Lydia*

# Disclaimer

This material is based upon work supported financially by the National Research Foundation of South Africa. Any opinion, findings and conclusions or recommendations expressed in this material are those of the author(s) and therefore the NRF does not accept any liability thereto.

Cambridge Elements ≡

# Twenty-First Century Music Practice

## Simon Zagorski-Thomas

*London College of Music, University of West London*

Simon Zagorski-Thomas is a Professor at the London College of Music (University of West London, UK) and founded and runs the 21st Century Music Practice Research Network. He is series editor for the Cambridge Elements series and Bloomsbury book series on 21st Century Music Practice. He is ex-chairman and co-founder of the Association for the Study of the Art of Record Production. He is a composer, sound engineer and producer and is, currently, writing a monograph on practical musicology. His books include *Musicology of Record Production* (2014; winner of the 2015 IASPM Book Prize), *The Art of Record Production: an Introductory Reader for a New Academic Field* co-edited with Simon Frith (2012), the *Bloomsbury Handbook of Music Production* co-edited with Andrew Bourbon (2020) and the *Art of Record Production: Creative Practice in the Studio* co-edited with Katia Isakoff, Serge Lacasse and Sophie Stévance (2020).

## About the Series

Elements in Twenty-First Century Music Practice has developed out of the 21st Century Music Practice Research Network, which currently has around 250 members in 30 countries and is dedicated to the study of what Christopher Small termed musicking – the process of making and sharing music rather than the output itself. Obviously this exists at the intersection of ethnomusicology, performance studies, and practice pedagogy / practice-led-research in composition, performance, recording, production, musical theatre, music for screen and other forms of multi-media musicking. The generic nature of the term '21st Century Music Practice' reflects the aim of the series to bring together all forms of music into a larger discussion of current practice and to provide a platform for research about any musical tradition or style. It embraces everything from hip-hop to historically informed performance and K-pop to Inuk throat singing.

Cambridge Elements ≡

# Twenty-First Century Music Practice

Printed in the United States
by Baker & Taylor Publisher Services